Writing and Life

Rock Folk
Boogie Lightning
How to Succeed in Show Business by Really Trying

Writing and Life

MICHAEL LYDON

University Press of New England

Hanover and London

Published by University Press of New England, Hanover, NH 03755
Printed in the United States of America

5 4 3 2 1
CIP data appear at the end of the book

for Ellen Mandel—

    the best first reader any writer ever had

CONTENTS

ACKNOWLEDGMENTS   *ix*

INTRODUCTION   *xi*

1. *The Art of Writing*   *1*

2. *Writing and Thought*   *25*

3. *Writing and the Self*   *45*

4. *Realism*   *59*

BIBLIOGRAPHY   *89*

ACKNOWLEDGMENTS

Terezhina Fonseca, Linda Bamber, Penny Liu, and my brother Peter Lydon all read and reread this essay in manuscript. I did my best to incorporate their countless excellent suggestions into the Patrick Press printing of two hundred copies in October, 1990.

Among many supportive readers, friends, and family, Peter Guralnick and my brother Christopher cheered me on with particular generosity. I owe heartfelt thanks to my mother, Alice Joyce Lydon, who has encouraged my writing since my elementary school efforts.

POLONIUS: —What do you read, my lord?
HAMLET: Words, words, words.

Shakespeare

I like reading and writing. The fun began with alphabet flash-cards in Mrs. Macomber's first grade—I remember distinctly the triumph of piecing "together" together for the first time—and has continued unabated for more than forty years.

In my big family—six kids—we wore the covers off *Winnie the Pooh* and *Now We Are Six*. Alice made me slightly seasick, but I ran and panted across the highland heath with Alan Breck Stuart and David Balfour in *Kidnapped* and, oh, that bloody battle in the roundhouse! In the fourth grade I swam and loafed with Huck and Tom and even tried to write my version of their immortal tale. In the fifth Natty Bumpo and I crept silently along Indian trails through the forests of old New York, and in the sixth I wandered lost down crooked London streets with Oliver Twist.

The nuns in junior high drilled us through old-fashioned sentence parsing; I "trotted" through Latin and Greek in high school except for one enthusiastic close reading of the First Book of Plato's *Republic*. Senior year Eustacia Vye tempted me with her curling kissable lips in *The Return of the Native*, and Becky Sharp bewitched me in *Vanity Fair*. Freshman year at Yale we read Chaucer, Milton, and Spenser with Professor Witherspoon, Ian Fleming in the dorms, and I went out for the *Daily News*. Sophomore year I wangled an interview with S. J. Perelman and, working that summer at the *Dayton Daily News*, read *War and Peace* in my boarding house. Hannah Arendt's sombre symphonic narrative in *The Origins of Totalitarianism* impressed me in poli sci, as did *Florian Geyer*, Gerhardt Hauptmann's close-up panorama of medieval war, in German class.

Through the rain and sunshine of the years since then, a book for the bus, a book before bed, browsed in a library, borrowed from a friend—books and writers, writers and books! Defoe and Dickens, Trollope and Eliot, Balzac and Dreiser; *The Charterhouse of Parma* and *Diary of a Country Priest*; the mysteries of Dorothy Sayers, Michael Innes, Rex Stout, and Agatha Christie; the short stories of Guy de Maupassant, O. Henry, Ring Lardner, and John O'Hara; *The Rise of Silas Lapham* and *A Modern Instance* by William Dean Howells; *Serenade* and *Mildred Pierce* by James M. Cain; everything by Raymond Chandler. I finished *The Brothers Karamazov* late one night and burst into tears.

All these books contain marvels, the most marvelous of which is this: how *real* they are! How packed with people I love and hate, how round with worlds that I trustingly enter. Writing, I find, does more than report life, sketch it in a static medium; writing *captures* life and, like a net thrown round a wild beast, writhes and snaps with the unsubdued energy of all it traps.

I wrote this essay to describe, succinctly yet in some detail, how writing tries to reach that goal. Using examples to illustrate my ideas, I first discuss a few of the art's most ancient techniques, go on to the thoughts of the writer at work, beyond that to the whole self that the writer invests in every sentence, and I conclude with realism—writing that succeeds in recreating life in word.

My ideas are those, not of a philosopher posing questions of meaning or a linguist analyzing language, but of a writer hoping to understand the work of colleagues and seeking a foundation for my own. Writing is a mirror in which we can see ourselves, and in writing about writing, the danger exists of going round in circles. I hope not to get lost in the riddle of this illusive double image, but to look into writing's mirror as a dancer looks into the mirror on her studio wall: to discover all she can learn to add to the grace of her dance.

This book is for everyone: for the writers who inspired me to write, for you, dear reader, and for me. Of the many motives that keep me at my desk, the greatest is the ambition to create work that, like the books I draw on for examples, will live on unshaken by passing centuries. The sum that reading has taught me is this: life is as it is, no matter the year. When writing tells that truth, it is true forever.

MICHAEL LYDON

JANUARY 1995

Writing and Life

CHAPTER I   ❧   *The Art of Writing*

Writing is the art of fixing words in sequence to convey thought from one human to another.

Writing weds two arts. A visual art, black ink on white paper, writing commands a host of graphic symbols. Letters— twenty-six in the English alphabet—spell the words, and a wide variety of marks punctuate them. These symbols are not drawings, but writing still connects to its ancient base in picture. Parentheses enclose words like two cupped hands, and capitals inform us of their importance by being big. Indeed, we recognize single words by seeing spaces between some letters and making a primitive visual judgment, "what looks together belongs together."

Writing is also an aural art; its symbols represent the sounds of speech. Breath vibrates our vocal cords to create the five vowels *a*, *e*, *i*, *o*, and *u*; our lips, teeth, tongue and palate work together to form the twenty-one consonants that introduce, connect, and close those vowels. Punctuation marks act as stage directions, indicating when to pause, stop, or change vocal tone. Many writers, myself included, "talk" our writing as we work, and any reader can turn writing into speech by reading it aloud.

Once wed, sight and sound may not be put asunder. We look and listen as we read, simultaneously experiencing speech as picture and picture as speech. Both elements of the art are crucial to its effect. We can create mental pictures from writing, for example, in part because we use our eyes to read. This—

> I looked up and saw a man at a window. He had a bushy beard, a lop-sided grin, and a hairy wart on the tip of his nose. He wore glasses and a stovepipe hat taller than Abe Lincoln's. As he looked back at me, he scratched his ear with a corncob pipe.

—becomes something like this in our minds as we read:

Our eyes scan back and forth across the word sequence as they would across the face of a real man, and as they do across this picture.

Of these twin elements, however, sound retains a certain primacy. Speech comes before reading and writing in human history, and in the history of most of us. I find writing a visible word music, more like singing than drawing. Writers use pen, ink, and paper as composers do: to record a sound sequence. As Beethoven's sharps and rests tell a performer what tones to play and how long to hold them, Balzac's letters and commas tell the reader how to sound words. The black rectangle of the printed page, framed and slashed by white, makes a pretty picture, but the pleasing look of letters serves to unlock a still greater beauty—the sound of words.

Ah, the beauty that words possess! A Frenchman, I understand, once said that he thought *cellardoor* the most beautiful word in English. *Cellardoor* connects three sound groups or syllables; many words have only one. All syllables have at least one vowel; most have one or more consonants too:

A, as, ash, mash, smash!

In words of several syllables, one is usually accented. There begins writing's rhythm:

*im*itate
im*meas*urable
imma*ture*

Any word repeated enough times becomes pure sound and quite silly: *good blood, bad blood, good blood, bad blood, good blood, bad. . . .* Many words, *rotund* and *thin*, for instance, seem to imitate in sound what they describe. Word sounds can create sharp contrasts—*smooth crack*—or link similarities in elision and alliteration:

Chattanooga choo choo
Woncha choo choo me home.

Rhyme strongly links like-sounding words. As its name suggests, rhyme's power depends on rhythm as well as sound similarity. In these lines—

> If you wish upon a star
> You are wishing very far.

—*star* and *far* rhyme, while the internal *are* rhyme is but a faint echo. Rhyme organizes words even when they have little other reason for being together. Lewis Carroll's rhymes make shaky sense of the Walrus's inconsequent conversation:

> "The time has come," the Walrus said,
> "To talk of many things:
> Of shoes—and ships—and sealing wax—
> Of cabbages—and kings—
> And why the sea is boiling hot—
> And whether pigs have wings."

When rhyme joins reason, sound supports sense, nowhere with more conviction than in the couplets with which Shakespeare ends his sonnets:

> But if the while I think on thee, dear friend,
> All losses are restored and sorrows end.

Word sense springs from word sound; we use our eyes to read, but the picture we form from writing comes, not directly from what we see, but from what we hear when we see. Seeing a word unlocks its sound, and sound sets off the symphony of word resonance—all the reverberant meanings a word has for us. "Uttering a word," Wittgenstein writes in *Philosophical In-*

vestigations, "is like striking a note on the keyboard of the imagination." If we read a single word we know—

China

—the sound of the word resounds in the echoing chambers of our minds, tripping flashes in a million brain cells, creating a vast assembled image of all the word means to us. Word resonance can take writing far beyond sight and sound; it connects words with all our senses. In that one word *China* we can not only see sights and hear sounds, we can taste tastes, smell smells, and touch a thousand silken textures. The word recalls taught facts and remembered faces. We sense in it the long history of a great race of mankind and a great portion of the earth. Sometimes we barely notice our experience of word resonance because we pass quickly on to the next word. If fancy strikes us, however, we can explore the broad avenues one word opens up, dwell on any aspect of its image and develop it in our imaginations—picturing the Great Wall clearly in our minds, for example, or remembering in detail a delicious Chinese meal.

Word resonance is word power. When words we know resound within us, they release all the energy packed into their seedlike shapes. Resonant words, harmoniously combined, toll in our minds like tuned bells. There are, for example, bees and clover, summer rain and sunshine, many tastes of golden sweetness in the word *honey*. *Milk* sings of cow and clover, mother and child, a warm barn on a winter night, and much, much more. Together, *milk and honey* ring with the happiness of a full and peaceful life. Conversely, in *death and destruction* we can hear all the din of hell.

When we write, we select the words we use—they are the

black we add to the white—but we cannot control the energy of word resonance. The language itself bestows this power on words; it is embedded in the histories of their birth, use, and association. Words, moreover, ring differently for each reader, depending on what each knows and feels. China may mean far more or far less to my neighbor than it does to me. When we do not know a word, it has no resonance for us. If, for example, I change one letter in China to make

Chona

—a possible word I don't recognize, my brain draws a blank, an experience writing represents as

?

Many words have ancient histories—Herodotus believed *mama* to be the oldest—but new words can be made up at will, and all words can be fixed in any sequence. *Pelgos neaf horse gas bomb zepud*—why not? To convey thought clearly, however, known words need to be used in sequences with recognizable structures. These structures, the architecture of writing, are described by the rules of grammar.

We may take pride in grammar as one of the great accomplishments of the human brain. Grammar's deepest roots may be biochemical, for it strikes me that grammar links words in sequence much as life combines molecules in strands to make up organic matter. Certainly studying grammar yields useful evidence on how our brains work, how we receive, understand, and use information. I think of grammar as the skeleton of thought; thought lives in grammar as flight lives in the bones of birds. Grammar turns thought into word, *logos* in ancient Greek. Grammar is logical.

The root structure of grammar is the sentence—"a group of words expressing a complete thought or feeling," as Norman Foerster and J. M. Steadman define it in their fine book, *Writing and Thinking*. From sentences grow paragraphs, from paragraphs grow chapters, and from chapters grow books. "Yes!" is a sentence, and so is "No." More often a sentence combines a thing—a noun—and an action—a verb—in dynamic unity:

Thing does

or

Thing is

Sometimes a thing does something by itself— "The clock ticks"; other times what the thing does affects something else—"the fire burns the wood." Things also *did* and *were*, and, we hope, *will do* and *will be*. Grammar has structures for all the faces of time. Christ declared a time beyond past and present in this pregnant sentence from the Gospel of St. John: "Before Abraham was, I am."

A sentence can describe things and actions with great exactitude. With this long word strand, Mark Twain describes Phelp's, a "one horse cotton plantation":

A rail fence round a two-acre yard; a stile made out of logs sawed off and upended in steps, like barrels of a different length, to climb over the fence with, and for the women to stand on when they are going to jump on to a horse; some sickly grass patches in the big yard, but mostly it was bare and smooth, like an old hat with the nap rubbed off; big double log house for the white folks—hewed logs, with the chinks stopped up with mud or mortar, and these mud stripes been whitewashed some time or another; round log kitchen, with a big broad, open but roofed passage joining it to the house; log smokehouse back of the kitchen; three little log nigger cabins in a row t'other side of the smokehouse; one little hut all by itself down against the back fence, and some outbuildings down a piece the other side; ash hopper and big kettle to bile soap in by the little hut; bench by the kitchen door with bucket of water and a gourd; hound asleep there in the sun; more hounds asleep round about; about three shade trees away off in a corner; some currant bushes and goose berry bushes in one place by the fence; outside of the fence a garden and a watermelon patch; then the cotton fields begin, and after the fields the woods.

The Adventures of Huckleberry Finn

With so few verbs, all those nouns are still in a hot Southern afternoon; the only action at Phelp's is a few hounds sleeping. In contrast, see how Dickens animates a blustery English night by packing these sentences from *Martin Chuzzlewit* with verbs and active nouns like *wind* and *pursuit*:

An evening wind uprose too, and the slighter branches cracked and rattled as they moved, in skeleton dances, to its moaning music. The withering leaves no longer quiet, hurried to and fro in search of shelter from its chill pursuit; the laborer unyoked his horses, and with head bent down, trudged briskly home beside them; and from the cottage windows lights began to lance and wink upon the darkening fields.

Read these two passages again. Isn't it remarkable how well these structured words make the scenes they describe real in our minds? Read the Twain, and there before us, as if we were leaning on the rail fence, drowses the Arkansas farm; the chill wind slicing through Dickens's Wiltshire village raises goose-bumps on our skin.

This is the art of writing's great triumph: writing can re-create life in word. Writing has the power to embrace all aspects of life, wrap them in logical strands of resonant words, and pin them on the printed page. Our oldest books record towering moments in the history of civilization:

> And she brought forth her firstborn son, and wrapped him in swaddling clothes, and laid him in a manger; because there was no room for them in the inn.
>
> And there were in the same country shepherds abiding in the field, keeping watch over their flock by night.
>
> And, lo, the angel of the Lord came upon them, and the glory of the Lord shone round about them: and they were sore afraid.
>
> And the angel said unto them, Fear not: for, behold, I bring you good tidings of great joy, which shall be to all people.
>
> For unto you is born this day in the city of David a Saviour, which is Christ the Lord.
>
> Gospel of Luke (2:7–11 KJV)

just as writing in the newspaper reports on the soon forgotten minutiae of the day-to-day:

IOWA ROUTS PURDUE BY 31–7

West Lafayette, Ind., Oct. 22 (AP)—Mike Saunders went 72 yards for a touchdown, and Tony Stewart raced 65 yards to set up another score as Iowa routed Purdue, 31–7, in a Big Ten Conference game today.

The Hawkeyes broke open the game in the second half, scoring three touchdowns on Saunders's run, an 11-yard Chuck Hartlieb pass to Deven Harberts and a 9-yard run by Richard Bass.

New York Times, Sunday, October 23, 1988

Writing can describe the life of the mind as well as it can that of the outside world:

His head felt rather dizzy; a sort of savage energy gleamed suddenly in his feverish eyes and his wasted, pale and yellow face. He did not know and did not think where he was going; he had one thought only "that all *this* must be ended today once for all, immediately; that he would not return home without it, because he *would not go on living like that*." How, with what to make an end? He had not an idea about it. He drove away thought; thought tortured him.

Dostoyevsky, *Crime and Punishment*

And it can capture moments when we are not sure which is which:

At the same time I remember, that the poor girl seemed to be yet telling her story audibly and plainly in my hearing; that I could feel her resting on my arm; that the stained house fronts put on human shapes and looked at me; that great water gates seemed to be opening and closing in my head, or in the air; and that the unreal things were more substantial than the real.

Dickens, *Bleak House*

Writing can describe the freest flights of imaginary life, like this bold march by a little man from the immortal land of Lilliput:

In a little time I felt something alive moving on my left leg, which advancing gently forward over my breast, came almost up to my chin; when, bending my eyes downward as much as I could, I perceived it to be a human creature not six inches high, with a bow and arrow in his hands, and a quiver at his back.

Jonathan Swift, *Gulliver's Travels*

It can describe the life of other writing—note the active verbs Walter Piston uses to describe this violin melody by Beethoven:

This curve rises from its lowest tone A to the high point B-flat, reached in the fifth measure, and it comes to rest on the C-sharp, a note in the lower half of its range of a ninth. The curve is a "wavy" curve, having the lesser points F and G as it ascends, and again the F in the seventh measure.

Walter Piston, *Counterpoint*

And, in the course of such descriptions, it can use its own logic constantly to check on how true the writing is to the life it describes:

Under this usage the statement: (Either) Jones is ill or Smith is away is true if Jones is ill and Smith is away, true again if Jones is not ill but Smith is away, true again if Jones is ill but Smith is not away, and false only in the case Jones is neither ill nor Smith away.

Willard Van Orman Quine, *Methods of Logic*

This ability to fix life in word is the essence of writing's value to humanity. Yet the art of writing also has limits. In two distinct ways it is not like the life it tries to capture. First, writing is words in sequence, one after another. Life, in contrast, is trillions of simultaneous events exploding in the headlong rush of expanding time. Second, words are symbols, not the actual things and actions they denote. Writing labels life, but surging life shakes off labels as Moby Dick shakes off harpoons. All writing, and indeed all human thought, are but a few of the infinite and intricate processes that we call the universe. Joyce Kilmer was quite right: "Poems are made by fools like me, Only God can make a tree."

Writing transcends these limits in three ways. The first is purely visual. Writers create their sequences word by word, but books are not printed in one continuous strand like tickertape. They are laid out with the sentences arranged in close parallel lines, just as in this essay. When we read, we follow the sequence, yet our eyes also skip ahead, bounce back, and see neighboring words and lines on the periphery. Valdimir Nabokov laments the writer's problem in *Lolita*: "I have to put the impact of an instantaneous vision into a sequence of words; their physical accumulation on the page impairs the actual flash, the sharp unity of the impression." Yet, as a reader, I find the quick series of images that follow Nabokov's complaint so closely packed on the page—

Rug-heap, car, old man-doll, Miss O.'s nurse running with a rustle, a half-empty tumbler in her hand, back to the screened porch—where the propped-up, imprisoned lady herself may be imagined screeching, but not loud enough to drown the rhythmical yaps of the junk setter walking from group to group—from a bunch of neighbors already collected on the sidewalk, near the bit of checked stuff, and back to the car which he had finally run to earth, and then to another group on the lawn, consisting of Leslie, two policemen and a sturdy man with tortoise shell glasses.

—That I see them all at once, just as did Humbert Humbert, Nabokov's narrator, when he rushes out of his house to find the wife he hates killed by a car.

Grammar provides the second and third devices to help writing leap the limits of sequence and label. These are *phrasing* and *metaphor*, and I find them two of the art's most ingenious tools. To see how they work we need to look back into the structure of a single sentence.

One sentence's complete thought, write Foerster and Steadman, "may contain any number of constituent thoughts," each a group of words within the sentence. Grammarians call such a subgroup a phrase; some phrases, depending on many factors, are called clauses. Here for example, is a simple sentence:

John fed Fido.

Adding a phrase, in this case a subordinate clause set off by commas, makes a complex sentence:

John, thinking of Betty, fed Fido.

The phrase's three words convey a new thought; equally important, the two commas add bounce to the rhythm and tone of the sentence melody. Now two pauses punctuate the beat of stressed and unstressed syllables:

> Bump (pause) *bump*bump bump *bump*bump (pause) bump *bump*bump.

The first pause marks a shift to a new tone of voice, the second a return to the original tone. "John . . . fed Fido" is the confident statement that spans the whole sentence; "thinking of Betty" is an inserted comment. The shift in tone matches the shift in the writer's point of view from eyesight to insight. The sentence's primary phrase reports the facts of what the writer sees; the subordinate phrase expresses an opinion of what is going on invisibly inside John's mind.

The overall effect of phrasing is exactly that of an actor whispering a stage aside, of a mother turning for a moment from chat with a neighbor to hush a child. Their pauses and shifts of tone convince us that the action we are watching is going forward on two different but simultaneous levels. Likewise, the phrasing of this sentence lets us know that John was feeding Fido and thinking of Betty at the same time.

Grammar includes countless phrasing devices, each shaping or turning, but never breaking, the onward flow of a sentence. *On one hand . . . on the other hand* balances two phrases; *either . . . or* contrasts two. *If . . . then* outlines an imaginary event in one phrase and posits a possible result in a second. *But* adds a phrase that takes off at an oblique angle from the one preceding: "John fed Fido, but Fido wasn't hungry." *Instead* introduces a phrase that the next phrase obliterates: "Instead of feeding Fido, John played chess."

With a descriptive phrase a writer can add to the visual picture of his sentence: "John, a sandy haired fellow of forty-two . . ."; a parenthetical phrase can publish what the writer privately thinks: "(and an utter fool in my humble opinion)." Since each phrase has its own tone and its own point of view, a sentence with many phrases becomes a complete thought presented in counterpoint by many voices from crisscrossing perspectives. In this gorgeously phrased sentence by Cervantes, I count three *if*'s, seven pauses, and ten phrases creating five points of view—Don Quixote's, Sancho Panza's, Dulcinea's, and those of the curate and the barber who are speaking:

> If his master should ask him, as he was bound to do, if he had delivered the letter to Dulcinea, Sancho was to say that, not being able to read and write, she had replied by word of mouth, her message being that her lover was to come to her at once, under pain of her displeasure if he failed to do so.
>
> *Don Quixote*

When grammarians analyze the structure of complex sentences like this one, they show the phrases branching off and running parallel to the sentence's central trunk. Foerster and Steadman even turn the diagram vertical to emphasize its treelike form:

As written, however, a complex sentence is still words in linear sequence just like a simple sentence. Phrases don't really branch off, they follow:

John, thinking of Betty, fed Fido.

Yet the grammarian's diagram makes sense because, as we've seen, the pauses and tonal shifts of phrasing create the illusion of simultaneity. The words "John, thinking of Betty, fed Fido" may walk in single file, but we experience them in parallel—

thinking of Betty,
John,   fed Fido.

—because the phrasing lets us know the two described actions happened in parallel.

Thus, while adding to writing's melodic lilt, phrasing gives the art the means to leap the limit of word sequence. The words still follow one-by-one, but the images they generate happen together in our minds just as events happen in life. Indeed, phrasing can do what life cannot: reverse a sequence of events. In the sentence—

Before John fed Fido, he ate his own dinner.

—the opening phrase describes action that happened after the action described by the closing phrase. Yet we can easily flip

John back to dining before he fed his dog because the phrasing tells us that what we read first happened second.

As phrasing helps writing over the sequence limit, metaphor helps writing over the limit of label. The English word *metaphor* comes from the Greek word *metapherein*, "carry over"; *transfer* is a synonym with Latin roots. In the widest definition of the word, all writing may be called metaphor, for this is what writing does: carry life over into written word, transfer reality to symbol. What empowers writing to do this is the traditional consensus writers and readers share: words may be taken as equivalents of fact. Once we agree that aspects of our experience can fairly be described with words—this is *house* and that is *horse*, this *walking* and that *talking*—we can then use those words as metaphors of reality to convey what we experience to others. So great is the transferring power of metaphor that in one word, *John*, we can see a whole human being, a fellow with a girlfriend and a dog. Fido, we may be sure, has fleas.

Metaphor in this sense of the word is the fundamental energy that writing draws on to create its lively world upon the page. When we arrange these reality transfers in strong grammatical structures—

John, talking to Fido, walked his horse to Betty's house.

—we can paint vivid pictures of life.

Yet if we define every word as a metaphor, metaphor is reduced to a label—a few pen strokes that sum up complex experience. And if all writing could do was to put these metaphors in fact-by-fact sequence, the procession of labels would be too dull to convey the full richness of life. Writing would stay hemmed in by the limits of its own labeling process, and the world it made would be as flat as the paper it is printed on.

Instead, writing leaps the limit of label by applying the power of metaphor to itself. If metaphor can make word equivalent to fact, then metaphor can make words, which are facts, equivalent to each other. A fine example of what I mean is the immortal metaphor Shakespeare gives to Romeo:

Juliet is the sun.

As labeling, this sentence is inaccurate. If John wrote it with the right labels on the right facts, it would read, "Betty is a woman." Juliet is also a woman, but by writing that she is the sun Shakespeare does more than label facts with words: he challenges us to contemplate a fascinating idea:

woman = sun

When we read the sentence, we hear the resonances of both words and do our best to equate them. If after comparison we agree with the Romeo—yes, a woman can be the sun to her lover—Shakespeare has succeeded in carrying the resonance of one word over into the resonance of another.

This is metaphor in grammar's more precise definition: writing's ability to transfer resonance word-to-word by equating different words in a sentence. Or, metaphor is the freedom to switch labels that comes with labeling. For words *are* labels and not the heavy things and arduous actions that they stand for; they are symbolic equivalents of those facts, images floating weightlessly in our minds before we set them down on paper. In writing, John can lift ten elephants as easily as he can Fido's dish because grammar, not gravity holds this world together, and grammar governs structure, not content. As long as a writer respects sentence structure, grammar allows free word substitution within a sentence, just as in the non-sense game of Fill in the Blank:

> "Betty washed her face and combed her . . ."
> "Potato!"

Metaphor used for sense is so common in writing that it can become nearly invisible. Writers often assume the reader knows how metaphor works and they leave its equation implicit. To find the metaphor in "Betty trampled on John's feelings," for example, we need to rewrite it: "Betty hurt John's feelings *as if* she walked on him with heavy boots." Cliches dull our awareness of metaphor by overuse; I have read the sentence "The Mideast is a powderkeg" too many times for it to explode any more in my mind.

Similes are metaphors where the equation is explicit but qualified by the words "like" or "as." Raymond Chandler often keeps a pace of a simile per sentence:

The light had an unreal greenish color, like light filtered through an aquarium tank. The plants filled the place, a forest of them, with nasty meaty leaves and stalks like the newly washed fingers of dead men. They smelled as overpowering as boiling alcohol under a blanket.

The Big Sleep

Proverbs are metaphors that convey time-tested principles of life in graphic images drawn from day-to-day problems: "Don't count your chickens before they hatch." Parables are extended similes that let us glimpse in homespun words great truths we may never fully grasp:

> The kingdom of heaven is like to a grain of mustard seed, which a man took and sowed in his field: which indeed is the least of all seeds: but when it is grown, it is the greatest among herbs, and becometh a tree, so that the birds of the air come and lodge in the branches thereof.
>
> Gospel of Matthew (13:31–32 KJV)

Fairy tales and fables use metaphor's magic power to change frogs into princes and pumpkins into golden carriages. A nightmarish metaphor is the heart of Franz Kafka's fantasy *Metamorphosis*: poor Gregor Samsa wakes up to find he has turned into an enormous cockroach. Allegory may be metaphor's most complex form, combining all the fanciful transfers of fable with the moral examples of proverb and parable. John Bunyan interlocks countless metaphors in his great allegory, *The Pilgrim's Progress*, creating a dream-like landscape of Delectable Mountains and Doubting Castles, populated by virtues and vices in human shapes. His magnificent fiend, Apollyon, is a patchwork quilt of similes:

> Now the monster was hideous to behold; he was clothed with scales like a fish (and they were his pride); he had wings like a dragon, feet like a bear, and out of his belly came fire and smoke, and his mouth was as the mouth of a lion.

In all its forms metaphor works the same way: the equation of two words equates two points of view on experience. Multiple metaphors like Bunyan's present a dizzying number of viewpoints, but a single metaphor like Shakespeare's "All the world's a stage" shows the two-way effect plainly. When we consider that sentence's proposition, *world equals stage*, we see all we can in the word *world*, all we can in the word *stage*, and then we try to resolve the two viewpoints in a single image, *the world as stage*.

Much of metaphor's power comes from the freedom it gives a writer to choose any two viewpoints. Since any two words may be equated, a writer may use metaphor to make the most free-form connections between disparate experiences. "Talking to John," for example, Betty could be "sitting on top of the world" or "down in the dumps"; she could feel excited "like a kid on Christmas morning" or "as lonely as a woman caught in a suffocating crowd." Charlotte Brontë is one of many writers who use metaphor to combine viewpoints on man and nature. Here she puts a human face on the heavens:

> She broke forth as never moon had yet burst from cloud: a hand first penetrated the sable folds and waved them away; then, not a moon but a white human form shone forth in the azure, inclining a glorious brow earthward. It gazed and gazed on me. It spoke to my spirit: immeasurably distant was the tone, yet so near it whispered in my heart—"My daughter, flee temptation!"
> *Jane Eyre*

And here she reverses the points of view to show animal forms underlying human dress:

> —I compared him with Mr. Rochester. I think (with deference be it spoken) the contrast could not be much greater between a

sleek gander and a fierce falcon: between a meek sheep and the
rough-coated keen-eyed dog, its guardian.

Jane Eyre

For all their potential variety, the many viewpoints of metaphor remain in essence two: fact and fancy. One side of the
equation describes experience literally or, we could say, labels
it correctly. The other side switches the label to describe the
same experience as interpreted by the human imagination.
Because metaphor is an equation, both viewpoints have equal
weight. In one pan of metaphor's scale Juliet is the woman
herself; in the other, she is the sun Romeo sees in his mind's
eye. Which is she more truly, woman or sun? Metaphor balances the two and declares she is truly both.

This ability to fuse fact and fancy makes metaphor one
of the principal techniques writing uses to recreate three-
dimensional life on two-dimensional paper. Metaphor acts
as writing's parallax, the two-sided vision of our eyes that,
when resolved by the brain, creates our picture of the spacious
world. As a navigator can triangulate the position of a ship far
at sea by viewing it from two separate points along the shore,
a writer can use the two perspectives of metaphor to triangulate life. The factual view complements the fanciful with the
firm structure of logic, the fanciful complements the factual
with the flexibility of imagination. Together, the two give writing the ability to render life word-by-word on a flat surface
and at the same time convey its incalculable depths.

Yet the power of metaphor, I think, cannot be fully ex-
plained as a writing technique. Metaphor is an impulse as
profound as any in human nature. "When Natives name white
men after animals,—the Fish, the Giraffe, the Fat Bull," Isak

Dinesen reports in *Out of Africa*, ". . . these white men, I believe, in their dark consciousness figure as both men and beasts." A white man known for years by an animal name through the "magic in words . . . comes to feel familiar with and related to the animal, he recognizes himself in it." Metaphor boldly asserts the value of the human mind. Every metaphor proclaims that as life seems to us, it is, that the universe within us is as vast as that without.

Metaphor, in sum, turns writing back from words to life. Used as labels, words substitute for experience; they give informative but pat answers to our questions about life. "Betty is a woman" tells us a person's gender but not who she is. In contrast, metaphor uses words to pose riddles; the answers it gives remind us that life is a mystery that words will never solve. "Juliet is the sun"—there is a paradox worth a lifetime of loving contemplation.

No writer knows better than Bunyan that the power of metaphor rests not in words themselves, but in the experiences they create. "By metaphors I speak," he writes in the eloquent "Apology" that introduces *The Pilgrim's Progress*. "I set my pen to paper with delight, quickly had my thoughts in black and white." Bunyan knows, however, that the lines he writes are not the sublime truths he hopes to describe. His lines, like a fisherman's, are the traps he sets to catch his elusive prey, aware, as any angler is, that "fish there be that neither hook nor line / Nor snare nor net nor engine can make thine."

What is true of metaphor is true of the entire art of writing. Resonant words and grammatical structures, musical phrases and magical metaphors—these are the art's great strategies in its heroic attempt to wrestle with life and pin it on the pages of a book. When by the most ingenious combination of these ploys writing does triumph, it must still bow before its never-to-be vanquished foe. For writing succeeds not by pointing us proudly to the page but by suggesting how we may look through the page to all that lies beyond. Or as Bunyan put it in yet another metaphor,

> My dark and cloudy words they do but hold
> The truth, as cabinets inclose the gold.

CHAPTER 2   *Writing and Thought*

Writing has the power to convey thought, to awaken thinking in the reader similar to the writer's own. In writing as in gift-giving, it is the thought that counts.

What is thought? How and why did it come to be? Who hopes to answer these ageless questions? Thought is vast: it is our memory of the past, the crest we ride in the action-packed present, our future ever expanding before us at the speed of light. For us humans, thought is all.

I can begin to grasp the vastness of thought by facing the here and now of my own experience. As I perceive my life, I sense I am always in a strong and continuously moving present, a *now* going forward into the new. I sense this motion in my own body, mind, and moods, and in the world and people around me. Life is always changing. Much of this change is cyclical, yet I see so many variations in even the most rhythmic of its cycles that I feel confident life, instead of endlessly repeating, is endlessly opening up new territory.

In this ever-changing present I know neither what will happen next nor what I'll do next. I do have a sense of what I'd like to happen and what I'd like to do. I try to make my life go in these directions. When things happen that I don't like, I act to minimize their effects. I react to change, in sum, by acting to improve the now or at least maintain a status quo I can accept.

Sometimes I win, sometimes I lose, and often I seem to leap from the frying pan into the fire.

I try to act in my own interest in a general way, working year after year to earn my living, for example, but what I want to point out here is that I do so in the most minute ways at every moment and at every level of my existence. I act to preserve and/or improve myself with every breath and every heartbeat. All the regulatory processes of my body chemistry are working to these ends. I act for myself in my instinctive actions—blinking to get dust out of my eye, throwing up my arm to ward off a hanging branch—and I certainly do so in all acts of preference. If I have the idea, "I'd like to go to the beach," I then go through the billions of acts necessary to get me there. When I'm ready to go home, I go. Then, "What's for dinner?" and afterward off to bed, up in the morning and back to work. In a word, I am always *now* facing *next*. This is life for me and, I think, for all of us whose minds are blessedly free from crippling illness or injury. May it go on for years to come!

Thought guides me in this mercurial moment. Since life is a continuous present of action and decision, I need constant answers to the constant question, "Now what? Now what?" Thought, I think, is the active force within me that comes up with the answers I need, that constantly suggests, "Try this, try that." Thought for me is more than what I consciously think and plan; it encompasses, too, my unconscious responses to changing life—all the habitual, instinctive, and biological adjustments I make continuously to keep on course with an even keel. Thought is my "devious-devising Odysseus"; without quite telling me what to do, thought creates the strategies I use to cope with the adventures of second-to-second life. Drawing on an age-old fund of remembered and ingrained experience, thought analyzes the tumultuous change I confront and, from the now's countless blended elements, synthesizes instant solutions. Thought gives me ideas about what to do next. Thought guides my actions.

For me, writing is an action. Proud as I am of my own writing, I know that, looked at without vanity, it represents but billions of my zillion actions. I push a pen, tap typewriter keys, and wield an eraser, just as I plump my pillow and shake pepper into my soup—to satisfy the need and desire of the moment. Every tap, every push, every erasure, is an answer to a "Now what?" Just like my in-between actions, when I scratch my head or get up to stretch my legs, my writing actions "seem like a good idea at the time." Years of practice have given me some control of the actions of writing, yet I often feel as clumsy as Charley, Esther Summerson's little maid in *Bleak House*. For most household tasks, Charley had "nimble little fingers," but—

> Writing was trying business to Charley, who seemed to have no natural power over a pen, but in whose hand every pen appeared to become perversely animated, and to go wrong and crooked, and to stop, and splash, and sidle into corners, like a saddle-donkey.

Thought guides the actions of writing as it guides our other actions. Nearly all writing is an act of preference, and thought guides it freely, letting the play of whim effect the work of steady purpose. Had Dickens, for example, thought it better to end that sentence with "balky pony" instead of "saddle-donkey," his hand, for an instant, would have traced different loops. For whatever reason, however, "saddle-donkey" was the word thought suggested and Dickens accepted, so he spelled out *s-a-d-d-l-e-hyphen-d-o-n-k-e-y*, and there it remains today in black and white.

Writing can convey thought because actions convey the thought that guides them. As we can see a man going to the beach and learn, "He thought of going to the beach," so, too, we can read what Dickens wrote and learn, "He thought of writing 'saddle-donkey.'" When thought suggests energetic motions to a writing hand, the ink the hand put on paper holds that guiding thought suspended, potential energy ready to animate the mind of a reader. In writing, thought paints a black and white self-portrait.

Many actions besides those of writing convey thought. We can see thought at work in all human busyness—the fads and fashions in what we wear, how we decorate our houses. The actions of all arts convey thought; music, dance, acting, painting, and sculpture do so without words. Beethoven and Balzac both scratched boldly with their pens, and both convey bold thought. The chiseled stones of the Acropolis speak the mind of ancient Greece as plainly as the printed pages of Plato's *Republic*.

Writers are artists who act frequently on the impulse to convey thought in word. Like their neighbors, writers have many thoughts they "hardly give a thought to," and few of these do they ever get around to writing down. Writers find conveying thought in word no easy task. "There is no way of writing well and also of writing easily," declared Anthony Trollope, who disciplined himself to write every day, no matter what. A writer conveys what he or she thinks; simply being aware enough of that to write it down takes paying close attention to thought as it happens. Thoughtful writing always conveys personal ideas and observation, although, of course, writers in full agreement can collaborate. The American Declaration of Independence, signed by fifty-six men, is an extraordinary example of this:

> We hold these truths to be self-evident,—that all men are created equal; that they are endowed by their creator with certain unalienable rights; that among these are life, liberty and the pursuit of happiness.

Every writer, moreover, faces a mind-boggling array of thoughts that could be written. A trivial incident on a boring day, a silly flicker of evanescent imagination, a solemn conclusion drawn from bitter lesson—all urge themselves into the mind, begging for the scrap of paper that confers immortality. Certain thoughts push themselves forward past other contenders, becoming more attractive for a host of reasons, aesthetic, practical, emotional, and economic; those are the thoughts that guide the body to the desk, the hand to the pen, and start it moving. What an infinite variety of thoughts have writers tackled through the ages! The skill and daring of these artists never ceases to move me, nor does the fertile power that motivates their work.

Even with one thought in mind to write, a writer must still find the words to convey it, and that labor has been the complaint of writers from time immemorial. Until fixed in word, thought darts like quicksilver from idea to idea, impishly ready to say whatever it pleases or, maddeningly, nothing at all. At times thought tantalizes the writer with words that are "on the tip of the tongue" but will not come to mind. At other times, thought presents so many ideas in so many words that the writer's problem is deciding which to use. Weavers who create cloth from the thread of thought, writers know the agony of its every tangled knot, the unruliness of its countless skeins of yarn!

Writing, in a word, requires thought. Fortunately, a writer need not lug this essential ingredient about like so many bags of raw material. Thought instead is a life-process reacting to change, an active force that helps the writer work. Thought grows in time, and the writer who can pace his efforts to match the growth of thought can, like a gardener who trusts in nature, halve his labor and double his output. Gardeners dig and manure the soil so their plants will flourish. Writers likewise cultivate thought as it sprouts and branches out from a germ kernel idea, and they too must wait until passing seasons turn blossoms into fruit.

Writing that grows with thought does more than describe life; it is itself alive. When a writer lets her pen trace thought's most impetuous zig-zags and most balanced symmetries, she animates logical form with life force. Word by word and sentence by sentence thought advances across the page like a vine creeping along the ground. The web of words becomes the skin of a thought, fleshed out by the energy of the thought itself. Foerster and Steadman call writing like this "organic," because it "assumes its proper shape as it develops itself from within." As Nathaniel Hawthorne hoped his own writing would, organic writing grows like grass.

This is what I call good writing, writing I love to read. Good writing conveys living thought with vibrant intensity. Each word in the sequence speaks its piece; no word is extra, none is out of place. Thought leaps like lightning from the words into my mind. Here the confidence of a man who relies utterly on God:

The Lord is my rock, and my fortress and my deliverer; my God in whom I will trust; my buckler and the horn of my salvation and my high tower.

David, Psalm 18

Here the self-loathing of a murderous king:

> What hands are here! Ha! They pluck out mine eyes.
> Will great Neptune's ocean wash this blood
> Clean from my hand? No, this my hand will rather
> The multitudinous seas incarnadine
> Making the green one red.

Shakespeare, *Macbeth*

And here the bleak vista before Lucifer, newly fallen to Hell:

> At once as far as Angels kenn he views
> A Dungeon horrible, on all sides round
> As one great Furnace flam'd, yet from those flames
> No light, but rather darkness visible
> Served only to discover sights of woe.

Milton, *Paradise Lost*

What thoughts are in these words! What passion in every syllable! The writers of these passages use words to open doors on thought's boundless depths, to paint kaleidoscopic visions with dazzling clarity. We can sense how far their thinking ranged in all that their few words bring home.

Thought vivid as this marks all good writing. Thought generates writing's words; thought guides the actions that inscribe them on paper. As it follows that no motion can be greater than its motive force, it follows that only living thought can make writing come alive. Certainly the genuine interest of the thought that writing conveys is a better measure of excellence than style considered as a quality apart from thought. Good writing comes in all styles. Henry Fielding's can be extravagantly florid:

> Hushed be every ruder breath. May the heathen ruler of the winds confine in iron chains the boisterous limbs of noisy Boreas, and the sharp-pointed nose of bitter biting Eurus. Do thou, oh sweet Zephyrus, rising from thy fragrant bed, mount the western sky, and lead on those delicious gales, the charms of which call forth the lovely Flora from her chamber, perfumed with pearly dews, when on the first of June, her birthday, the blooming maid, in loose attire, gently trips it over the verdant mead, where every flower rises to do her homage, 'till the whole field becomes enamelled, and colors contend with sweets which shall ravish her most.
>
> *Tom Jones*

Lawrence Sterne's absurdly inconsequent:

> Let us go back to the ********—in the last chapter. It is a singular stroke of eloquence (at least it was so when eloquence flourished at Athens and Rome, and would be so did the orators wear mantles) not to mention the name of a thing, when you had the thing about you *in petto*, ready to produce, pop, in the place you want it. A scar, an axe, a sword, a pinked doublet, a rusty helmet, a pound and a half of pot-ashes in an urn, or a three-halfpenny pickle pot—but above all, a tender infant royally accoutred. —Tho' if it was too young, and the oration as long as Tully's second Philippic—it must certainly have beshit the orator's mantle.
>
> *Tristram Shandy*

and Dashiell Hammett's as taut as the split-second decisions of a desperate man:

> The room had two windows. He went to the nearer window and tried to raise it. It was locked. He unfastened the lock and raised the window. Outside was night. He put a leg over the sill, then the other, turned so that he was lying belly-down across the sill, lowered himself until he was hanging by his hands, felt with his feet for some support, found none, and let himself drop.
>
> *The Glass Key*

These examples demonstrate, however, that style is not a quality apart from thought, but its voice, and what matters is that its tone and color suit the thought it speaks. If a style is well-wedded to vivid thought, that style will be well-written. Lifeless or boring thought, on the other hand, cannot be well written. Dullness has a leaden vocabulary, narcissism a pompous one. I much prefer interesting ideas lurking half-hidden in a clumsy style to glib ones posing in faultless refinement. The anonymous student who wrote this famous howler—

> Napoleon stood with one food in the Ancien Regime, and with the other he saluted the rising sun of 19th century democracy.

—made Napoleon look cockeyed, but he did have an idea worth considering.

Good writing, in sum, conveys vivid thought in vivid words. This is the goal any writer worthy of the name is always trying to reach. Lining up his words as a general lines up his troops, he sends them into battle on the page, ordering them to stand and fire when they see the whites of a reader's eye. When the reader understands the thought the writer hopes to convey, victory is won. Foerster and Steadman quote a Roman orator: "Write not that your reader *may* understand if he will, but that he *must* understand, whether he will or no." Like a comedian telling a joke, the writer wants the reader to "get it." Here, for example, Mark Twain wants us to get that Huck didn't get Buck's story about Moses and the candle:

> . . . and he asked me where Moses was when the candle went out. I said I didn't know; I hadn't heard about it before, no way.
>
> "Well, guess," he says.
>
> "How'm I going to guess," says I, "when I never heard tell of it before."
>
> "But you can guess, can't you? It's just as easy."
>
> "Which candle?" says I.
>
> "Why, any candle," says he.
>
> "I don't know where he was," says I; "where was he?"
>
> "Why, he was in the *dark*! That's where he was!"
>
> "Well, if you knowed, what did you ask me for?"
>
> "Why, blame it, its a riddle. . . .
>
> *The Adventures of Huckleberry Finn*

That writing can convey thought is easily proven. If I ask you, dear reader, to clap your hands, and you clap, you have received and responded to thought conveyed by writing. Readers alone with a book are often moved to laughter or to tears. Some, when they put the book down, get up inspired to go in directions they otherwise never would have taken.

History provides countless examples of how influential written thought can be. To take one: Thomas Paine published *Common Sense* in January 1776 when the American colonies, though at war with England, had not agreed on the ultimate goal of the conflict. In ringing sentences Paine called for all

Americans to make their goal the "RIGHTS of MANKIND, and of the FREE AND INDEPENDENT STATES OF AMERICA," and declared these thoughts common sense:

> Now is the seed time of continental union. . . . Everything that is right or reasonable pleads for separation. The blood of the slain, the weeping voice of nature cries, IT IS TIME TO PART. . . . Ye that dare oppose not only the tyranny but the tyrant, stand forth! . . . A government of our own is our natural right. . . .

Over a hundred thousand copies of the sixty-page pamphlet spread quickly through the colonies, acting on the public, according to one historian, "like an electric shock." In March, George Washington wrote from Virginia that *Common Sense* was "working a powerful change . . . in the minds of many men." When copies arrived at a rebel camp in Massachusetts an officer observed that "a reinforcement of five thousand men would not have inspired the troops with equal confidence." "As many as read, so many become converted," reported a British newspaper. That spring the thirteen colonies united around a single word: independence; by the 4th of July the thoughts of *Common Sense* had become the consensus of a new nation.

When we read and understand, we learn what another human thinks. Humans therefore have made writing a primary medium of communication, trusting it as a tool for teaching and for the safekeeping of our history. As a medium and storehouse for thought, writing has many advantages. It can be accurate, true in detail to fact and nuance, and it is versatile: no subject is beyond its grasp. Writing is imperishable. The paper and ink of its first edition return in time to dust, but the words can be reprinted. Writing is economical. A slim volume can hold a treasury of ideas. Even after a worldwide holocaust, we could begin to reconstruct civilization if one library of moderate size were left standing.

Writing has only one limit as a medium of thought: reading depends on an acquired knowledge of a language's symbols and grammar. Without that knowledge, we cannot decipher the thought the writing conveys. Once lost, the key that unlocks thought in written language can be difficult to find. The key to Egyptian hieroglyphics, for example, was lost about 400 A.D., and until Jean François Champollion deciphered them in 1822, the tomb inscriptions of the pyramids were as silent a riddle as the Sphinx.

For most readers, not knowing how to read the many languages in active use is more of a problem than finding the key to a lost language. I can tell, for example, that these lines of Hindi:

क्योंकि ईश्वरने जगतको ऐसा प्यार किया कि उसने अपना एकलौता पुत्र दिया कि जो कोई उसपर विश्वास करे सो भ्राष्ट न होय परन्तु अनन्त जीवन पावे।

are writing, but I cannot read them. Writers face the same problem in reverse: how can we convey thought to the millions of readers who do not understand the language we write in?

The nonverbal arts suffer less from this language-to-language limit than writing does. Music, dance, acting, painting, and sculpture are each in their own way languages, and their symbols and grammar vary widely among the many cultures of the earth. My first time at a shadow play in Sumatra I might not know why an audience laughed when it did, just as a Sumatran might not get all I do from a jazzman improvising on the blues. By my fifth time at the shadow play, however, I think I would have learned much simply by watching, listening, and trying to understand; whereas I could stare at that passage in Hindi from now to Doomsday and still not have a clue to its thought.

Why? Because the symbols and grammar of the nonverbal arts are more universally understood than those of writing, and we can unlock the thought they convey by looking for universals that underlie cultural difference. Music everywhere, for example, conveys thought and feeling with sound and silence, tone and tempo. Dance and drama condense their languages from the expressive gestures of all mankind: a jump is a jump in Germany or Japan, so too are a grin or a grimace, a man and woman parting or embracing. Painting and sculpture have age-old conventions recognized by the entire species. Who does not know instantly that these three are human beings?

(a)   *(b)*   *(c)*

There is no such skeleton key to unlock the many written languages of the world. Despite similarities and historical connections, each language develops its symbols and its grammar on its own. The correspondence between thought and symbol in writing is arbitrary compared to the same correspondence in the nonverbal arts. In English, for example, we could spell *smile f-r-o-w-n* if we wished, either by giving the letters *f-r-o-w-n* the sounds we now give *s-m-i-l-e,* or by giving the sound *frown* the resonance we now give to *smile.* Making these changes might be pointless and difficult, but there is nothing in the symbols themselves that says we may not. In contrast, we cannot switch the symbols of the nonverbal arts with similar impunity, for a smile looks like this:

a frown looks like this:

and the whole world knows it.

Writing, however, can leap its language-to-language limit with translation. A writer who knows two written languages translates one into another by rewriting the first in the symbols and grammar of the second. The Hindi passage above, for example, is a translation of this sentence from the Gospel of St. John:

> For God so loved the world, that he gave his only begotten Son, that whosoever believeth in Him should not perish, but have eternal life.
>
> Gospel of John (3:16 KJV)

This sentence, in turn, comes from the King James translation of the Bible into English from Hebrew, Aramaic, and Greek. I find translation a most valuable tool. With it I can receive the thought of writers in every language, and hope that my thought will one day be understood around the world.

Some writers, it is worth noting, think translation does not work. Once thought and word are wedded in writing, they believe, different words cannot convey the same thought. Foerster and Steadman argue the point succinctly. "There are not various ways of saying the same thing," they write in *Writing and Thinking*; therefore, there are no translations . . .":

> There are so called "translations," to be sure, but on account of the organic unity of thought and expression, they necessarily fail to reproduce exactly the author's meaning. The only way to read Homer is to read Homer. . . .

Translation does attempt to cross daunting boundaries. "Babel is a very profound notion," the well-known modern translator Richard Howard said in a recent *New York Times* interview; "there are days when translation does seem impossible, when the English word 'bread' and the French word 'pain' seem to be only absurd equivalents."

I think, however, that translation is possible—there *are* various ways of saying the same thing. Thought does not give up its freedom when fixed in word; it gains the freedom to play on countless new minds. I rest this conviction on four broad beliefs.

First, I believe that writing serves thought, not the other way around. Thought, as we've seen, is our problem solver, our "devious-devising Odysseus"; writing is one of thought's most ingenious solutions to the problem of communication. If communication between two written languages becomes a problem, thought can solve that too. Thought, in a word, knows more than one way to skin a cat. I see ample evidence of this in the satisfactory use of translation everywhere, everyday. In New York City, for example, the transit authority does not want subway passengers to lean against the train doors, so they post this sign in English:

DO NOT LEAN AGAINST THE DOOR

Many New Yorkers, however, read only Spanish, so they put up this sign too:

NO SE APOYE CONTRA LA PUERTA

The Spanish sentence with it's reflexive "se" and feminine "la puerta" is a touch more intimate than the impersonal English one, but observation tells me that Spanish and English readers all get the single thought the transit authority hopes to convey, and that they heed and ignore it in equal measure.

Second, life is too tumultuous for the art of describing it in word to be an exact science. Thought gives writing rich resources of synonym and alternate phrasing so it may approximate life's multiplicity as best it can. Scarlet, crimson, ruby, rose, and vermilion—each word conveys a shade or red, but there are reds best described as being "somewhere between magenta and maroon." Between many synonyms I find no discernable difference. If a man walks across a room with notable determination, one witness might write, "John strode across the room," and another write, "John walked vigorously across the room." Here is a possible French translation: "Jean a traversé la chambre vigoureusement." These sentences are all different, and their descriptions incomplete, yet I find no reason but taste to choose between them. They all convey the same thought because all describe the same event with equal accuracy.

Third, I believe that readers translate what they read into

their own personal language. Receiving conveyed thought is a dynamic event: the writer's thought enters and reacts with the reader's. Sometimes a line or two is so apt and in tune with a reader's own thought that it's swallowed whole and becomes a favorite quotation. Far more often readers forget the words they read, remembering only the gist as they would express it themselves. This internal translation is more than an accidental by-product of reading; it is proof that thought has successfully been conveyed. As every teacher knows, a student has learned a subject when "she can put it into her own words."

Readers have put the greatest works of literature "into their own words" countless times; many of their translations are now part of each work's enduring monument. Readers have not only rewritten the Bible, Homer, Shakespeare, Cervantes, and Dickens in all the languages of the world, they have also turned them into plays, operas, novels, and films; poems, paintings, sculptures, symphonies, and stained-glass windows. These translations are new works of art, not exact copies, yet I find it striking how much they do convey of the written thought that inspired them. Michelangelo's marble *Pietà*, Picasso's sketches of Don Quixote and Sancho Panza, Olivier's filmed *Henry the Fifth*—I think these extend the thought of their originals far more than they distort it. In many cases we know the translation as well or better than the first writing. I am one of the millions who cannot help seeing Leonardo Da Vinci's *Last Supper* in these lines from the Gospel of St. Mark:

And his disciples went forth . . . and they made ready the passover.

And in the evening he cometh with the twelve.

And as they sat and did eat, Jesus said, "Verily I say unto you, One of you which eateth with me shall betray me.

And they began to be sorrowful, and to say unto him one by one, Is it I? and another said, "Is it I?

Gospel of Mark (14:16–19 KJV)

Fourth and finally, I believe I understand the thought of the great writers I read in translation. Translation, at least, puts no greater limit on my understanding than my own ability. Perhaps I do know *Sister Carrie* better than I know *Cousin Bette*. Like Dreiser, I am an American; I daily walk the streets that Carrie walked. Life, however, may someday take me to live in Paris; then I will know Balzac's world more closely than I do today.

Yet I get Balzac now, as I get Aristophanes and Sophocles, Cicero and Lucretius; Molière, Hugo, and Zola; Dostoyevsky, Tolstoy, and Solzhenitsyn. When I read a good translation of good writing, the English is lively, idiomatic, and makes perfect sense. I know the original was in a different language, and as I read, I sense intriguing foreign flavors. Thought vivid in Russian is still vivid thought in English, and I have no more trouble seeing this Russian carriage bowling along through summertime Pavlovsk:

> . . . a magnificent carriage, drawn by two white horses, suddenly dashed by the prince's house. Two gorgeous ladies were sitting in it. But after driving no more than ten paces past the house, the carriage stopped; one of the two ladies turned around quickly, as though she had suddenly caught sight of a friend she wanted to see.
>
> Dostoyevsky, *The Idiot*

than I do seeing these English horses pulling the Dover Mail up Shooter's Hill one murky night in late November:

With drooping heads and tremulous tails they mashed their

way through the thick mud, floundering and stumbling between whiles as if they were falling to pieces at the larger joints.
As often as the driver rested them and brought them to a stand,
with wary "Wo-ho! so-ho-then!" the near leader violently
shook his head and everything on it—like an unusually em-
phatic horse, denying that the coach could be got up the hill.

Dickens, *A Tale of Two Cities*

Indeed, whenever I read and understand, I feel I am seeing
another person's thought as through a window. When the
window is crystal-clear and thought presses through it with
the intense interest of an ever-changing landscape, I become
so absorbed in all that I see that I forget I am looking through
a window. This, I think, is the miracle of writing: writing
conveys thought mind-to-mind as if it were not there at all.

Yet writing is there, a window of words, made of ink and
paper. I can keep the physical fact of writing firmly in mind
only when I look at writing I cannot read. Then, by virtue of
being opaque, the window is all I can see. In museums I have
bent over glass cases to study tablets of cuneiform writing
from ancient Sumeria. Because this writing presses its thought
at me in vain, I can see plainly that writing is not thought pure
and simple, but the trace of a human hand guided by thought.
Every triangular indent proves that once a scribe pushed,
lifted, turned, and pushed his stylus again and again into the
then soft clay. His actions, like mine, took place in the continuously moving present; like mine, his actions were among
his zillion on-the-spot answers to life's constant question,
"Now what?" Of all this long-ago writer thought, his writing
tells me only this for certain: that he thought then, as I do now,
"*Write!*"

CHAPTER 3 ❧ *Writing and the Self*

> It happened one day about noon going towards my boat, I was exceedingly surprised with the print of a man's naked foot on the shore, which was very plain to be seen in the sand. I stood like one thunder-struck, or as if I had seen an apparition; I listened, I looked around me, I could hear nothing, nor see anything; I went up to a rising ground to look around farther; I went up the shore and down the shore, but it was all one, I could see no other impression but that one.

When Robinson Crusoe came thus upon the spoor of his fellow man after fourteen years alone, Daniel Defoe tells us, he ran home to his hut, "terrify'd to the last degree," and barred himself in against the unknown intruder. Like that single footprint, all writing is proof positive: a human was here. Every time we read, we follow a trail blazed by a writer. Used as we are to daily intercourse with our neighbors, we may be less wary than the solitary Crusoe, but as we track a writer's inky step across the snowy page, we too want to know, "Who goes there?"

Writing is more than artful sequence and interesting thought; it is the mark of a human self. What is the self? What makes you you and me me? Is there a point where thought ends and the self begins? Unanswerable questions all! I experience my life as one person. Thought and self are two aspects of this single being, and the difference I sense between them is, briefly, this: thought suggests, the self decides. Of many things I think of doing, I choose the things I do. The self is the active being in me, and in all of us, who chooses to act on some of the options thought suggests. It follows that we reveal who we are by what we do. No writer is more eloquent on this than Emerson. If we take his word "character" as a synonym for "self," this passage conveys my idea exactly:

> Human character evermore publishes itself. The most fugitive deed and word, the mere air of doing a thing, the intimated purpose, expresses character. If you act you show character; if you sit still, if you sleep, you show it.

> What [a man] is engraves itself on his face, on his form, on his fortunes, in letters of light.

> Concealment avails him nothing, boasting nothing. There is confession in the glances of our eyes, in our smiles, in salutations, and in the grasp of hands. . . . —all blab.
>
> *Spiritual Laws*

We can readily observe that no two people act alike in all that they do. That is strong external proof that we all have different selves. From within we all know that each of us is a vast galaxy: "I am all I know and remember, imagine and experience." And we know a gulf as well as a bond exists between ourselves and neighboring galaxies: "I am like others, but no one else *is* me."

To reach these other selves, we send signals with our voices, faces, hands, and whole bodies. We learn about others from the signals they send to us. Every signal conveys a message from a self hoping to be understood. Sometimes gesture gets the message across directly; sometimes gesture molds matter into telling shapes or signs that embody the intended message. We shout, jump up and down, curl our lips, shrug our shoulders, or trace our darting hand—

—all to say to other selves, "Hello, this is *me*, this is what I think."

In this context, writing is one of many human sign languages. Whenever humans meet—Crusoe and Friday, for instance—countless signals begin to flash back and forth in complex conversation. Most are fleeting, cut to the need of each succeeding moment. We rely on their accuracy yet can be fooled by clever mimicking. We delight in or are annoyed by their uncanny precision in conveying what a person is like: "The way you wear your hat!" Sometimes we don't understand another's signals and feel how clumsy and approximate our own attempts to convey ourselves can be.

Writers often describe the teeming exchange of signals that makes up human social life. Here Dostoyevsky describes the body language of four nervous people:

Ferdyshchenko could not keep still; Rogozhin looked on bewildered and kept looking at the prince and Pitsyn with terrible uneasiness. Darya Alexeyevna seemed unable to bear the suspense much longer. Even Lebedev was unable to restrain himself, came out of his corner, and, craning his neck perilously, began peering over Pitsyn's shoulder at the letter, with the air of a man who was afraid of getting a sound thrashing then and there for doing so.

The Idiot

Here Michael Innes describes the mysterious language of the eyes:

Meredith had forgotten the girl who had appeared to be sitting on the desk, and who had slumped so swiftly and quietly into a chair. But he looked at her attentively enough now. And the girl looked equally attentively at him. It was only for a moment. But what passed between them was full of obscure intimations. "Ah, yes," said Meredith softly—and more than ever before his whole soul, for some reason, went into sustaining his sinister role.

From London Far

And no writer is more adept than Jane Austen at catching the competitive counterpoint of drawing room dialogue:

"I did not know before," continued Bingley immediately, "that you were a studier of character. It must be an amusing study."

"Yes, but intricate characters are the *most* amusing. They have at least that advantage."

"The country," said Darcy, "can in general supply but few

subjects for such a study. In a country neighborhood you move in a very confined and unvarying society."

"But people themselves alter so much, that there is something new to be observed in them forever."

"Yes, indeed," cried Mrs. Bennet, offended by his manner of mentioning a country neighborhood. "I assure you there is quite as much of *that* going on in the country as in the town."

Pride and Prejudice

With each signal a self attempts to create and communicate a physical equivalent of what it is experiencing—an image that will convey the whole being at that moment. The immediate thought that inspired the signal looms large in the image's content; age, sex, racial and cultural heritage, emotional mood, circumstance, and time of day, year, and era all contribute trace elements, many of which the sender and receiver, fish in their own water, barely notice. Sometimes the receiver picks up aspects of the signal that the sender hopes will not be noticed:

Though his letter was full of Mr. Crawley and his affairs there was not a word in it about Grace. This, however, was quite natural. Major Grantly perfectly well understood his father's anxiety to carry his point without seeming to allude to the disagreeable subject. "My father is clever," he said to himself, "very clever. But he isn't so clever but one can see how clever he is."

Anthony Trollope, *The Last Chronicle of Barset*

All the arts, writing included, are signal-sending and image-making studied, perfected, and powered by intense concentrations of human energy. An artist is one more self signaling and hoping to be understood, and he or she, like others, often feels like a helpless bumbler at the task. To gain control over signal-sending, artists practice and experiment endlessly. Their goal is such mastery over movement that every gesture clearly communicates its message. In performance, artists move before our eyes and ears; otherwise they record movement in a medium, and we experience their movements through that. What composer Roger Sessions wrote of music is true of all the arts, live and recorded:

> In embodying movement, in the most subtle and most delicate manner possible, it communicates the attitudes inherent in and implied by that movement.
>
> *The Musical Experience*

Artists learn to control gesture so as to communicate attitude in its subtlest shades. One who receives these gestures, Sessions continues, in time "gets a clear sense of a quality of feeling behind them." That "clear sense of a quality of feeling" is, I think, knowledge of another self. Compared to the quick-sketch signals of everyday, an artist's images are jewels painstakingly cut and buffed, but all the more are they self-images. The lustre that draws our eye has but one source: the light in the eye of the artist.

An artist may explore the most distant and timeless realms of his galaxy, but, like his earthbound neighbors, he has only his body and his lifetime, gesture and the moment, with which to report his findings. The recording arts, writing included, attempt to leap that limit. Artists gesture to make a mark on some material, hoping that the "quality of feeling" animating the gesture, the self at that moment, will live on in the mark when the moment is gone. They do not hope in vain; Walt Whitman *is* with us every time we read his long, loose lines:

I am with you, you men and women of a generation or ever so
many generations hence;
I project myself—also I return—I am with you, and know
how it is.

Just as you feel when you look on the river and sky, so I felt;
Just as any of you is one of a living crowd, I was one of a crowd;
Just as you are refresh'd by the gladness of the river, and the
bright flow, I was refreshed;
Just as you stand and lean on the rail, yet hurry with the swift
current, I stood, yet was hurried.
Just as you look on the numberless masts of ships, and thick
stem'd pipes of steamboats, I looked.

Crossing Brooklyn Ferry

When we see an artist's mark, we reanimate the artist by
coming to a growing conclusion as to who would mark just so.
Each mark is a clue we can read in the manner of Sherlock
Holmes, who needed but one glance when they first met to
know that Watson was a doctor who made house calls on
foggy London nights:

"It is simplicity itself," said he; "my eyes tell me that on the
inside of your left shoe, just where the firelight strikes it, the
leather is scored by six almost parallel cuts. Obviously they
have been caused by some one who has very carelessly scraped
around the edges of the sole in order to remove crusted mud
from it. Hence, you see, my double deduction that you had
been out in vile weather, and that you had a particular boot-
slitting specimen of the London slavey. As to your practise, if a
gentleman walks into my room smelling of iodoform, with a
black mark of nitrate of silver upon his right forefinger, and a
bulge on the side of his top hat to show where he had secreted

his stethoscope, I must be dull indeed, if I do not pronounce him to be an active member of the medical profession."

A. Conan Doyle, *A Scandal in Bohemia*

Every particular of an artist's mark is packed with information about the artist's self. The details and the overall form, the style and the content, are all revealing choices. Capable artists need only a little black and white to present themselves vividly. Here is Rembrandt:

Saskia at an Open Window. Rotterdam, Boymans-van Beuningen Museum. Drawing. Reprinted from Jakob Rosenberg, *Rembrandt* (Cambridge: Harvard University Press, 1948).

here is Ogden Nash:

> The Ostrich roams the great Sahara.
> Its mouth is wide, its neck is narra.
> It has such long and lofty legs,
> I'm glad it sits to lay its eggs.

and here Shakespeare:

> To be or not to be, that is the question.

Who is Shakespeare? Any conclusion must grow by leaps and bounds to keep abreast of the quick self in this great artist's mark. As we track his pointed pen, we race a still more pointed wit. "His hand and mind went together," write John Hemmings and Henry Condell, fellow actors who edited the First Folio. Thomas Carlyle finds in Shakespeare's writing "such calmness of depth; placid joyous strength; all things imagined in that great soul of his so true and clear, as in a tranquil unfathomable sea!" Yet Shakespeare too is a man open as a savage to the pressing panoply of all nature, capable of hurling into a hurricane words of equal force:

> Blow, winds, and crack your cheeks!
> Rage! blow!
> You cataracts and hurricanoes, spout
> Till you have drench'd our steeples, drown'd the cocks!
> You sulphurous and thought-executing fires,
> Vaunt couriers to oak-cleaving thunderbolts,
> Singe my white head!
>
> *King Lear*

Shakespeare's mark reveals that Shakespeare loves his native England, its language and its soil, its plants and animals, its people, place, and history. He is a fine craftsman in his trade and knows the theatre, stage and pit, as well as any man before or since. He loves a good joke and can tell one too. He loves men and women and knows us to our marrows. Romeo and Juliet, Beatrice and Benedick, Falstaff and young Hal, the drunken porter in *Macbeth*, boasting Glendower, black Richard—these characters are who we humans are, "not modified by the customs of particular places, unpracticed by the rest of the world," as Samuel Johnson writes in his magnificent *Preface to Shakespeare*, but "the genuine progeny of common humanity such as the world will always supply, and observation will always find."

As a writer, Shakespeare is without peer. "The source of his strength," writes Carlyle, "is a calmly seeing eye, a great intellect."

> The thing he looks at reveals not this or that face of it, but its inmost heart and generic secret: it dissolves itself as in light before him, so that he discerns the perfect structure of it. Creative, we said poetic creation, what is this too but *seeing* the thing sufficiently? The *word* that will describe the thing follows of itself from such clear intense sight of the thing.
>
> *Shakespeare*

Words spill from Shakespeare's pen electric with life, ringing like all the bells of London. What sentence does not tell his skill? I found these two robust examples by opening the pages as they fell—here the red-hot wrath of a betrayed king:

> What shall I say to thee, Lord Scroop, thou cruel,
> Ingrateful savage, and inhuman creature!

Thou that didst bear the key of all my counsels,
That knew'st the very bottom of my soul,
That almost might have coined me into gold,
Wouldst thou have practised on me for thy use,
May it be possible, that foreign hire
Could out of thee extract one spark of evil
That might annoy my finger? 'tis so strange,
That though the truth of it stands off as gross
As black and white, my eye will scarcely see it.

Henry V

and here Cassius, bitterly sarcastic:

Come, Antony, and young Octavius, come,
Revenge yourself alone on Cassius,
For Cassius is aweary of the world;
Hated by one he loves; braved by his brother;
Checked like a bondsman; all his faults observed,
Set in a notebook, learn'd, and conn'd by rote,
To cast into my teeth. O, I could weep
My spirit from my eyes! There is my dagger,
And here my naked breast; within, a heart
Dearer than Plutus' mine, richer than gold:
If that thou be'st a Roman, take it forth;
I, that denied thee gold, will give my heart:
Strike as thou didst at Caesar; for, I know,
When thou didst hate him worst, thou loved him better
Than ever thou lovedst Cassius.

Julius Caesar

Shakespeare's "facetious grace in writing," as his publisher
contemporary Henry Chuttle put it, flowed so freely that Ben
Jonson, much as he loved his rival's "excellent phantasy, brave

notions, and gentle expressions," felt "sometimes it was necessary he should be stopped." Shakespeare's fecund composition remains a wonder to all writers. "The work of a correct and regular writer," writes Samuel Johnson, "is a garden accurately formed and diligently planted, varied with shades and scented with flowers." Shakespeare's work, in contrast, "is a forest"—

> in which oaks extend their branches, and pines tower in the air, interspersed sometimes with weeds and brambles, and sometimes giving shelter to myrtles, and to roses; filling the eye with an awful pomp and gratifying the mind with endless diversity. Other poets display cabinets of precious rarities, minutely finished, wrought into shape, and polished into brightness. Shakespeare opens a mine which contains gold and diamonds in inexhaustible plenty, though clouded by incrustations, debased by impurities, and mingled with a mass of meaner minerals.

Shakespeare reveals so much in his extraordinary mark that centuries of unwearied scholarship have but begun to enumerate it. The accumulation of attitudes inherent in his gestures is indeed immense. Remember, however, all the words he wrote flow from a single self, a human like you and me. This self is the genius that glows like a golden smile in the stage lights every time his work is played. "For executive faculty, for creation, Shakespeare is unique," Emerson writes. "No man can imagine it better. He was the farthest reach of subtlety compatible with a single self."

Shakespeare is a writer great enough to stand for all writers: as we may know Shakespeare through his mark, so may we know all writers through theirs. When a writer looks life in the face and records what he sees, as Shakespeare did, the self that sees and writes lives in the writing. This is the voice that beguiles us to read. We are being called by another galaxy. Through the grille of words on the page is a person as real, enormous, silly, bright and cloudy as myself, and he is talking to me:

In sum, we can know a writer through his writing, the man through the paper mask. The writer is not us because we did not and could not mark just so; he is like us because when we read and understand his mark, we see it can be so. Can we know a writer perfectly? No, and neither can we know perfectly our next door neighbor. Is a writer friend or foe? To know that, read and decide for yourself!

For me, good writers are good friends, and good friends are good fortune. Ever ready to catch my eye, writers entertain me through hours of fair and foul weather, sharing thoughts that thrill and inspire me, telling stories of wonderful people in fascinating places. The webs they weave become hammocks in which I lie back with utmost trust while they sing charming melodies in word. The ideas and pleasures they give challenge and cheer me, the joys and sorrows they relate convince me they know my own. I value their written marks as I treasure the homely and revealing ways of those I truly love.

The deepest appeal of writing for me is the knowledge and love I gain of another self, the writer through the words. From books, writers I know and love enter my heart, there to dwell, I hope, as long as I live. My good friend Shakespeare speaks my own conviction:

> Let me not to the marriage of true minds
> Admit impediments, love is not love
> Which alters when it alteration finds,
> Or bends with the remover to remove.
> O no, it is an ever-fixed mark
> That looks on tempests and is never shaken;
> It is the star to every wand'ring bark,
> Whose worth's unknown, although his height be taken.
> Love's not Time's fool, though rosy *lips* and *cheeks*
> Within his bending sickle's compass comes.
> Love alters not with his brief hours and weeks,
> But bears it out, even to the edge of doom:
> > If this be error and upon me proved,
> > I never writ, nor no man ever loved.

> Sonnet 116

CHAPTER 4

✻ *Realism*

Writing that describes believable imaginary life I call realism, yet realism, I often need to remind myself, is an illusion. In the world of sticks and stones, writing is but ink on pressed fiber, and a book no more than a paper brick, good for propping open a window. Only in the world of words does Mr. Pickwick ride the coach from London to Rochester; Anna Karenina never lived that she could kill herself under the wheels of a train.

A writer creates the illusion of realism with the sequence of words: we read words and see imaginary events as if they actually happened. The illusion rests on two pairs of assumptions, shared by writer and reader, that together support realism as stout poles brace painted backdrops in a theater.

The first pair are the assumptions of reporting: *there is a world we all know*, and *writing can describe it*. For example:

It is a sunny afternoon in late winter. Outside my window the stalks of last year's flowers shiver in the cold West wind. Across the street a man walks by, his head tilted back to look at the sky. Another man walks down the middle of the street opening a knapsack as he goes.

Here I am reporting my own direct observation as truly as my skill with words permits. You may believe it as you would any reliable eyewitness account, for the passage paints a selective but accurate picture of what I saw. I call writing like this realistic writing. Its pair of assumptions makes possible the writing of news and history, biography and autobiography, texts of scientific description and technical information. The value of realistic writing depends on how well its words accord with facts. A history book that declares Galileo discovered America in 1066 is as useless as a geography book that says rivers run upstream.

Realistic writing is the spine of realism. Realism depends on its close connection with life to convince the reader that the sequence of words relates a sequence of plausible facts. Yet realism also reports on imaginary life. To add this "unreal" dimension, realism needs the second pair of assumptions, the assumptions of make-believe. These are: *words create their own world*, and *that world is whatever the words say it is*. For example:

> The city lay locked in blue flame as raindrops streaked from bone-dry streets to the blood green sky. Three giraffes smoked ice cubes and talked baseball. A man with nine legs and one enormous ear said, "No one's coming home yesterday." The city became a small purple pea pod.

Here I am *not* reporting observation; I wrote this passage sitting at my desk and made it preposterous on purpose. Yet look how real these words make these ludicrous events. When we read them, the words resound with us, and thought does its best to paint a picture from them—even if that picture has no factual equivalent. You may never have seen ice-cube-smoking giraffes before, but now you can! This is imaginative writing, whose pair of assumptions makes possible all story-telling—fiction, fable, fantasy, and fairy tale. The value of imaginative writing depends on the pleasure it gives the reader. No matter how far-fetched, a tale that readers enjoy serves its purpose.

Realistic and imaginative writing contrast, yet realism blends the two in seamless unity. As the former is realism's spine, the latter is its spirit of play. The first pair of assumptions attaches writing to life, the second pair detaches it. Realistic writing keeps realism's feet on the ground of what did happen; imaginative writing lets realism leap into the magical realm of metaphor where anything can happen. For example:

> "And here," said Great Aunt Matilda, entering the parlor, "is my greatest treasure, the Ming vase dear Arthur brought me from Peking. Priceless, of course, and the sentimental value."
>
> "Oh, yes," Mary said dutifully.
>
> Just then a red rubber ball bounded into the room followed by Mary's chubby son John running with his baseball bat. Crash! went John into the vase, smashing it into a thousand pieces.

This is realism. It is as believable as the scene written from direct observation and as make-believe as the one written from imagination. The characters, action, and place sketched in this example never existed, but they could have: they are unreal but possible. Readers may paint in the details of the scene differently; words like *Ming vase* and *great-aunt* resound individually. But all readers will be able to agree on the scene's essential elements because we all share the four assumptions on how words work and on what life is like. Writing can describe real and imaginary life equally well. When writing describes imaginary life that, except for being imaginary, could be real, that is realism.

Realism can vary the proportions of the realistic-imaginative blend over a wide range. In the example above, for instance, I could change the Aunt Matilda to Queen Elizabeth and Arthur to Prince Philip; then the passage is a fictional moment in the lives of real people. Or a maid could come in crying, "President Kennedy's been shot, I heard it on the radio," thus attaching the fiction to a real day in history, November 22, 1963. I could go in the other direction and make Matilda Queen Zotha and Arthur Prince Plegar who brought back a sacred zaponar from Planet Alforg. With an animal metaphor I could make them all frogs in a pond deep in the Lost Forest; or I could leave them humans as they are but let magic enter their lives:

> Suddenly the pieces of the vase began to whirl in the air until they melted into the shape of a smiling Chinese genie who bowed low before the astonished John.
>
> "Master, how may I serve you?" intoned the genie.

All such realism blends the four assumptions. The most realistic is still imaginary, the most imaginary still described as if it were real. The central illusion of my example stays the same in all blends: we read words and see two adults watching a child break a valuable object as if we too were eyewitnesses. As long as the writing makes that illusion believable, it is realism. Calling Matilda Elizabeth, Zotha, or Granny Frog is simple word substitution, a question of taste in metaphor. Something precious is being smashed—that is the illusory action whether we call the thing a vase, zaponar, or crystal lily pad.

For the moment let us stick with Matilda, Mary, and John. I could end my story there or jump to another scene, leaving the reader in suspense with the vase's flying fragments. If I continue, what next? Matilda could scream with horror or be speechless, have a heart attack or sob with relief at the release from a secret burden. Mary could protect or punish her child, and John could laugh, cry, or run away. Any number of next sentences could continue the realism. I could also continue:

> "Now let's have some tea," said Aunt Matilda, settling herself comfortably on the sofa. "Have a watercress sandwich, they're delicious."

Unless that is a clue to Mary and the reader that poor old Matilda has gone deaf and blind, the writing is no longer realism: Matilda wouldn't ignore her treasure being smashed! The words still follow each other matter-of-factly on the page, but the illusion they create no longer rests securely on either pair of assumptions. In the world of words the writing is illogical; in the world of fact it is not true to life.

The illogic begins with the denial of word resonance. "Treasure," "priceless," and "sentimental value" all convey that the destruction of anything so described would matter deeply to its owner. If Matilda doesn't care that John broke the vase, she is denying her description of it a moment before. This denial makes the dramatic structure of the scene illogical: an explosive cause has no effect. The opening of the scene sets a premise: Matilda loves her vase. Her next actions show she doesn't love it. This B doesn't follow its A; it contradicts A. This structural logic creates emotional illogic: Matilda doesn't continue to act as the person we first met would act. As actors say, she breaks character.

The sum of these illogics is that the picture the writing paints is not lifelike. I find it harder to visualize than the wildest fantasy—even on Planet Alforg the loss of something dearly loved would be a major event. My mind refuses to bridge the gap between the breaking vase and Matilda's oblivious response. As I read, I question the scene's reality. My answer is, "No, people don't act like that, it's not the way life works."

Writing like this I call unrealism. Unrealism is common: periodical pieces that puff celebrities of the moment; novels in which characters tread along the box-like lanes of the writer's outline; mysteries in which detectives catch murderers with mechanically placed clue sentences instead of logical deductions from believable facts; books written as copies of other books in stereotyped genres; and romances in which adoring heroines live only for dream heroes who take inhuman punishment without a whimper. Unrealism smothers word resonance in the fog of its own vagueness. Its rickety structures have a momentary plausibility and then collapse; its characters are all glitter and no gold. Unrealism is writing's chaff; its insubstantial nature ensures that, once read, it is soon forgotten. For, being weak in observation and imagination, unrealism is weak in graspable details. By being weak in detail, it is hard to believe; and by being hard to believe, it is hard to remember. Whether the product of shallow vision or poor workmanship, unrealism is writing that at best is half-alive.

Realism, in contrast, embraces life and wrests from it imperishable art. Or tries to do so, for all realism attempts to answer a daunting challenge: write to make the imaginary real and the real imaginary; create a world of words that can be seen as plainly as we can see the world around us; weave an illusion both factual and fanciful, lifelike and logical, believable and beguiling. Many who attempt realism fail, and no writer can be utterly sure of success.

A realist is a writer who keeps trying no matter what. Like a man stalking a wild horse in an open field, a writer holds no more than a rope of words, and even as he steps softly toward the defiant beast, he wonders how he'll ever bridle a stallion with such a paltry piece of string. To throw the lariat and miss may mean a fall in the dust, a kick in the head, but success, ah, a headlong ride clinging to a tangled mane!

Reckless courage, therefore, is a necessary ingredient in a realist's makeup. He needs also, I think, three other human qualities. A realist must *observe* life keenly, *imagine* life boldly, and *write well*.

The most important of these three qualities is observing life keenly. For a realist, life is the great subject, an everflowing spring of ideas and information, endlessly fascinating just as it is. Deaf to the sirens who urge dressing up every lily with a little bit of gilt, a realist will scan the dullest prospect until the stones of a dead-end street give up their secrets. A Parisian strolling through the Rue Neuve-Sainte-Geneviève in 1819, wrote Balzac, "would see nothing but cheap boarding houses and institutions, poverty and ennui." Yet in just the dining room of one such boarding house, the immortal Maison Vauquer in *Père Goriot*, Balzac sees chipped carafes on sticky buffets, piles of blue-bordered porcelain plates, the boarders' napkins in numbered pigeonholes, and he makes the reader see them too:

You can see a barometer furnished with a capuchin monk who pops out when it's raining; some engravings quite ghastly enough to take away your appetite, all with varnished wooden frames sporting gold stripes; a hanging wall clock in a scalloped case, inlaid in leather; a green stove; some of Monsieur Argand's eighteenth century gas lamps (but with the oil heavily larded with dust); a long table covered with oilcoth so greasy that, if a waggish diner wanted to, he could write his name in it, using nothing more than his finger as a pen; an assortment of variously maimed chairs; some tattered reed mats, always falling apart but never finishing the job; plus some miserable charcoal foot-warmers, foot-holes broken, hinges destroyed, wooden fittings all charred away.

Realists frame their art on forms they observe in life. Where does a story begin and end? What is its central line, where does it curve and climax? Realists answer these questions by looking at life. Imagination supplies the details of what the characters do as individuals; what happens to us all gives structure to the tale. "Chapter One. I am born," Dickens begins David Copperfield, letting David tell the story of his own life to date, a story any of us could tell about ourselves. Theodore Dreiser builds his great *Trilogy of Desire* on the lifespan of one character, Frank Cowperwood, American capitalist, from birth in pre-Civil War Philadelphia to death in a New York hotel suite early in the twentieth century. John Galsworthy overlaps dozens of such spans in *The Forsyte Saga*, following the fortunes of one family through succeeding generations. In contrast, Alexander Solzhenitsyn rests *A Day in the Life of Ivan Denisovich* on a far shorter span: one human from first waking to last drifting thoughts before sleep:

Shukov went to sleep, and he was very happy. He'd had a lot of luck today. They hadn't put him in the cooler. The gang hadn't been chased out to work in the Socialist Community Development. He'd finagled an extra bowl of mush at noon. The boss had gotten them good rates for their work. He'd felt good making that wall. They hadn't found that piece of steel in the frisk. Caesar had paid him off in the evening. He'd bought some tobacco. And he'd gotten over that sickness.

Nothing had spoiled the day and it had almost been happy.

There were three thousand six hundred and fifty three days like this in his sentence, from reveille to lights out.

The three extra ones were because of the leap years. . . .

Realists observe and describe men and women in love more than any other life-form. Over centuries they have found sexual magnetism the most dependable bond to hold their plots together. Few tales have more twists than *The Odyssey*, but Homer states Odysseus's goal in the first lines—home with his wife on Ithaka—and, devious as the wily one's trail is, to Penelope's arms he is always headed. Lovers step through the intricate dance of human courtship in countless stories, and the battle of the sexes provides the primal conflict for comedies and tragedies of equal number. The reasons why this form predominates lie too deep in the human heart to be summed up here. Suffice it to say that love fascinates us all. Readers devour love stories in print as avidly as they listen to gossip over the back fence. The greatest challenge realists face is to convey sex in all its passionate hues and delicate flavors. Here Shakespeare shows how traces of combat linger teasingly in playful moments.

Romeo: Lady, by yonder blessed moon I swear
           That tips with silver all these fruit-tree tops,

Juliet: O! Swear not by the moon, the inconstant moon,
      That monthly changes in her circled orb,
      Lest that thy love prove likewise variable.

Romeo: What shall I swear by?

Juliet: Do not swear at all; . . .

                Romeo and Juliet, Act II, Scene 2

Realists observe life playing havoc with human hopes and plans. They often use natural disasters, coincidental meetings, and chance twists of fate as hinges to swing their stories in new directions. In *The Return of the Native*, for example, Thomas Hardy shows how Clym Yeobright and Eustacia Vye might have lived happily ever after like so many literary lovers but for two slight errors. Timothy Fairway first forgets to deliver Clym's letter to Eustacia begging her to come back; then when he does remember and gives it to Captain Vye, Eustacia's grandfather, the Captain, seeing no light under Eustacia's bedroom door, mistakenly concludes she is asleep: "he ought not to disturb her; and descending again to the parlor, he placed the letter on the mantelpiece to give it to her in the morning." Alas, the morning would be too late. Not hearing from Clym, Eustacia slips out in the night and drowns herself in the circular pool of Shadwater Weir.

A bold imagination is a realist's second most important quality. Imagination becomes most obvious at the fantastic end of realism's spectrum, when the realist uses metaphor to create and inhabit worlds that exist nowhere else but on the page—Ray Bradbury's Mars, for example:

They had a house of crystal pillars on the planet Mars by the end of an empty sea, and every morning you could see Mrs. K eating the golden fruits that grew from the crystal walls, or cleaning the house with handfuls of magnetic dust which, taking all the dirt with it, blew away on the hot wind. Afternoons, when the fossil sea was warm and motionless, and the wind trees stood stiff in the yard, and the little distant Martian bone town was all enclosed, and no one drifted out of doors, you could see Mr. K himself in his room, reading from a metal book with raised hieroglyphs over which he brushed his hand, as one might play a harp.

The Martian Chronicles

Yet imagination is equally present in the most prosaic realism, when the realist uses words as plain labels to create human characters right here on earth:

Mrs. Glegg had both a front and a back parlour in her excellent house at St. Ogg's. . . . From her front windows she could look down Tofton Road, leading out of St. Ogg's, and note the growing tendency to "gadding about" in the wives of men not retired from business, together with a practice of wearing woven cotton stockings, which opened a dreary prospect for the coming generation; and from her back windows she could look down the pleasant garden and orchard which stretched to the river and observe the folly of Mr. Glegg in spending his time among "them flowers and vegetables."

Eliot, *The Mill on the Floss*

All realism springs from the imagination; imagination makes up the whole story, beginning to end. Even the most realistic realists insist that the fiction they create is not real. James Jones, for example, begins *Go to the Widowmaker* with a detailed version of the standard disclaimer:

This novel is a work of fiction and any resemblance to any real people, living or dead is completely coincidental, and totally outside the author's intention. The characters are not real people; they belong entirely to the author, who created them slowly over a long period of time, with a great deal of anguish and parental care, and also with a great deal of love.

—though *Go to the Widowmaker* tells the adventures of Ron Grant who, like Jones, is a stocky and successful writer from the American Midwest.

If is the imagination's springboard word, two letters that build all the castles in Spain. Realists commonly use four *if*s to create imaginary life: "*What if these people lived?*" "*What if this place existed?*" "*What if the impossible were possible?*" and "*What if we knew everything?*"

Every realist uses the first if: it gives birth to the fictional characters whose lives all realism relates. Fictional characters are among the most superb of human inventions. Each generation creates its own, and the most vital live through succeeding generations until they float deathlessly in the mind of mankind, a vast population of ghostly but beloved figures— Melville's Ahab for one:

He looked like a man cut away from the stake, when the fire has overrunningly wasted all the limbs without consuming them, or taking away one particle from their compacted aged robustness. His whole high, broad form seemed made from solid bronze, and shaped in an unalterable mould, like Cellini's cast Perseus. Threading its way out from among his grey hairs, and continuing right down one side of his tawny scorched face and neck, till it disappeared in his clothing, you saw a slender rod-like mark, lividly whitish.

Melville, *Moby Dick*

Realists use "*What if this place existed?*" less universally, their characters often walking well-known streets in real cities. They nearly always, however, invent details of such locales, specific houses and interiors, and they frequently coalesce the features of many similar real places into one fictional place. "Kyauktada was a fairly typical Upper Burma town," George Orwell writes in *Burmese Days*:

> The native town, and the courts and the jail, were over to the right, mostly hidden in green groves of peepul trees. The spire of the pagoda rose from the trees like a slender spear tipped with gold. . . . In 1910 the Government made it the head-quarters of a district and a seat of progress—interpretable as a block of law courts, with their army of fat but ravenous pleaders, a hospital, a school and one of those huge durable jails which the English have built everywhere between Gibraltar and Hong Kong.

In *The Shining* Stephen King not only invents the Overlook Hotel as an imaginary place, he makes it a character, the book's archvillain who dies by fire:

> The furnace exploded, shattering the basement's roofbeams, sending them crashing down like the bones of a dinosaur. The gasjet which had fed the furnace, unstoppered now, rose up in a bellowing pylon of flame through the riven floor of the lobby. The carpeting on the stair risers caught, racing up to the first floor level as if to tell dreadful good news. A fusillade of explosions ripped the place. . . . Flame belched out of the Overlook's five chimneys at the breaking clouds.
>
> (No! Mustn't! Mustn't MUSTN'T!)

It shrieked; it shrieked but now it was voiceless and it was only screaming panic and doom and damnation in its own ear. . . .

To make the Overlook a character, King uses the third if, "*What if the impossible were possible?*" Imagination can run riot with this *if* of fantasy. Homer uses it to invent the Cyclops, a race of one-eyed giants; H. G. Wells to build a machine that can travel backward and forward in time, and F. Scott Fitzgerald to mine a diamond as big as the Ritz. Some realists eschew the *if* of fantasy, agreeing with Cervantes that "the more truthful a book appears, the better it is as fiction, and the more probable and possible it is, the more it captivates." Yet the age-old popularity of fairy tales is proof enough of this *if*'s magic charm. Realists who write fantasy do their best to convince the reader that the impossible may be possible after all. E. B. White, for example, bases his delightful *Charlotte's Web* on the premise that barnyard animals can talk and even write like humans. Eight-year-old Fern Arable regularly eavesdrops on their conversations, sitting on a milking stool by the pigsty. Her mother thinks this is nonsense and asks the family doctor, "Dr. Dorian, do you believe animals talk?"

"I never heard one say anything," he replied. "But that proves nothing. It is quite possible that an animal has spoken civilly to me and that I didn't catch the remark because I wasn't paying attention. Children pay better attention than grownups. If Fern says that the animals in Zuckerman's barn talk, I'm quite ready to believe her. Perhaps if people talked less, animals would talk more. . . ."

The fourth *if*, "*What if we knew everything?*," creates what some critics call the "omniscient author," but what I call moveable point of view. Realists use the other *if*s to create characters and the worlds they inhabit; this *if* creates a fluid vantage point from which to view that world. When a realist uses a moveable point of view well, writer and reader, delightfully invisible, step together into a bubble-like space capsule that whisks us about, taking us anywhere we need to go to follow the unfolding story. Floating utterly unseen by the characters, we watch them when they hide:

> At last when the unknown was mounting to the fourth floor, [Raskolnikov] suddenly started, and succeeded in slipping neatly and quickly back into the flat and closing the door behind him. Then he took the hook and softly, noiselessly, fixed it in the catch. Instinct helped him. When he had done this, he crouched holding his breath, by the door. The unknown visitor was by now also at the door. They were now standing opposite one another, as he had just before been standing with the old woman, when the door divided them and he was listening.
>
> Dostoyevsky, *Crime and Punishment*

And we slip into their minds to eavesdrop on their unspoken thoughts:

> . . . Emma sat down to think and be miserable. It was a wretched business indeed. Such an overthrow of everything she had been wishing for. Such a development of everything most unwelcome. Such a blow for Harriet! That was the worst of all. . . .
>
> "If I had not persuaded Harriet into liking the man, I could have borne anything. He might have doubled his presumption to me—but poor Harriet!"
>
> Jane Austen, *Emma*

A master of moveable point of view like Anthony Trollope can cruise us through the minds and pockets of a man and woman dancing without missing a beat:

> It was all very sweet, that dancing with her, as they used to dance, without any question why it was so . . . but this would not further his views. The opportunity had come to him that he must use, if he ever intended to use such opportunity. There was the two hundred pounds in his pocket, which he did not intend to give back. "Does it put you in mind of 'old days?'" he said.
>
> The words roused her from her sleep at once, and dissipated her dream. The facts all rushed upon her in an instant: the letter in her pocket; the request she had made to Alice. . . .
>
> *Can You Forgive Her?*

When Vronsky's horse breaks her back in *Anna Karenina*, Tolstoy first takes us close to Vronsky on the steeplechase track:

> . . . he stood staggering alone on the muddy, stationary ground and Frou-Frou lay breathing heavily before him, bending her head back and gazing at him with her beautiful eyes. Still unable to realize what had happened, Vronsky tugged at the rein. Again she writhed like a fish, creaking the flaps of the saddle, put out her forelegs but, unable to lift her back, immediately collapsed and fell on her side again.

then to the grandstand with Anna where we see the same event in longshot:

Without replying to her husband, Anna lifted her binoculars and gazed toward the place where Vronsky had fallen; but it was so far off and so many people had crowded there that it was impossible to distinguish anything.

Realists do not always use moveable point of view. Some, like Raymond Chandler, stick rigorously to the "I" of first-person point of view—what a narrator experiences and discovers:

I went over and picked the gun up and wiped it off very carefully and put it down again. I picked up the three rouge-stained cigarette stubs out of the tray on the table and carried them into the bathroom and flushed them down the toilet. Then I looked around for the second glass with her fingerprints on it. There wasn't any second glass.

The High Window

Yet moveable point of view is a tool of tremendous imaginative power. With it realists can create action not only from the events described, but also from the writer's and reader's motion as they zoom around those events trying to get the best possible view. I know no more dynamic example of this than the early chapters of *The Hunchback of Notre Dame*. Hugo first takes us down to the smoky depths of Paris's thieves' kitchen, the Cour des Miracles:

Fires, round which swarmed strange-looking groups, were blazing here and there. All was bustle, confusion, uproar. Coarse laughter, the crying of children, the voices of women, were intermingled. The hands and heads of this multitude, black upon a luminous ground, were making a thousand antic gestures. A dog which looked like a man, or a man who looked like a dog, might be seen from time to time passing over the place on which trembled the reflection of the fires, interspersed with broad ill-defined shadows.

Then, at a constantly accelerating pace, Hugo leads us into Notre Dame and up the towers of the great cathedral until we come out on the roof and have a bird's-eye view of the entire city in sunlit panorama:

The spectator, on arriving breathless at that elevation, was dazzled by the chaos of roofs, chimneys, streets, bridges, belfries, towers, and steeples. All burst at once upon the eye—the carved gable, the sharp roof, the turret perched upon the angles of the walls, the stone pyramid of the eleventh century, the slated obelisk of the fifteenth, the round and naked keep of the castle, the square and fretted tower of the church, the great and the small, the massive and the light.

These four *ifs*, however, are less crucial to realism than observation of life. Looking back over the examples just above, I am more struck by their observant quality than I am by their purely imaginative quality. The K's may live on Mars, but they are a couple in a house near a town just like the Gleggs. Ahab, Raskolnikov, and Anna Karenina are characters born in the imagination of Melville, Dostoyevsky, and Tolstoy, but they grow to greatness because these realists pour into them all they know of what makes us humans tick.

Imagination is the spark that gets realism's motor running; observation is the motor that carries the fiction through long-running plots and hundreds of passing pages. In logical terms, imagination creates the premise, and observation determines the consequence. E. B. White's "animals can talk" premise, for example, gets *Charlotte's Web* going, but what follows is what White thinks would happen next given what life is like. Imagination sets White's stage and brings on his players; observation supplies how they will act in their imaginary circumstances. If White's observation is weak or deficient, his writing will soon become unreal. As it is, White observes and renders rural life with loving accuracy. When Charlotte the spider writes "SOME PIG" in her web over Wilbur's pigsty, for example, Wilbur becomes so famous that the Arables decide to show him at the county fair. Here the family pulls into the fair grounds:

> . . . they could hear music and see the Ferris wheel turning in the sky. They could smell the dust of the race track where the sprinkling cart had moistened it; and they could smell hamburgers frying and see balloons aloft. They could hear sheep blatting in their pens. An enormous voice over the loudspeaker said: "Attention, please! Will the owner of Pontiac car, license number H-2439, please move your car away from the fireworks shed!"
>
> "Can I have some money?" asked Fern.

When Wilbur wins the grand prize, Fern's ten-year-old brother gets soaking wet in the excitement before the grandstand:

> . . . of course Avery was tickled to find himself so wet, and he immediately started to act like a clown. He pretended he was taking a shower bath; he made faces and danced around and rubbed imaginary soap in his armpits. Then he dried himself with an imaginary towel.

"Avery, stop it!" cried his mother. "Stop showing off."

But the crowd loved it. Avery heard nothing but the applause.

These scenes are as imaginary as Avery's soap and towel, yet they become real because we sense how deeply and directly White observed them from life.

Writing well is the third requirement for any aspiring realist. Some writers might say this last should be first, for the sequence of words alone conveys the living thought that is realism. All realists face the practical task of composing that sequence. "I turn sentences around," novelist E. I. Lonoff tells the eager apprentice Nathan Zuckerman in Philip Roth's *The Ghost Writer*, "That's my life. I write a sentence and then I turn it around. Then I look at it and I turn it around again. Then I have lunch." No matter what a realist observes and imagines, he or she must describe it in words to be a realist or a writer at all.

Realism must be well-written because writing's sequence of words *is* a slender thread. It can lasso untamed life, but only if spun and plaited with the closest attention to the strength of every strand, the logic of every link. Realism demands full use of all of writing's resources, sound as well as sense. Realists must be attuned to word resonance and responsive to word rhythm, must phrase sentences with musical clarity and color descriptions with evocative metaphor. The writing must grow word by word and sentence by sentence, yet must not rush forward unchecked; thought needs to be organized into paragraphs and to breathe between chapters; narrative needs the contrast of action and repose. No matter how serious the subject, realists must brighten it with humor so the reader will be entertained enough to keep reading. As hard as they work to let the characters speak for themselves, they must let their own voice be heard. The realist can afford to scant not a single aspect of the art of writing; success demands, at a minimum, that every line be well crafted.

All the quotations in this book demonstrate the good writing that realism demands. By now I hope you realize how much I love good writing and esteem the skill of writers who create it. Yet I still put *writing well* third after *imagination* and *observation*. For, again, writing serves thought; we value writing because it can convey one human's thought into another mind with all its wit and dash intact. Observation and imagination, as aspects of thought, partake of its restless and spontaneous nature; writing is but the patient scribe that sets down black and white reminders of those spots where thought lingered briefly before moving on. Observation and imagination do not determine writing's every word; writing has its own ideas of the best way to say things, and sometimes masters must bow and be conveyed as their servant arranges. Yet observation and imagination are the twin forces that bring life to writing, and realism packs writing with life.

Abstract argument cannot separate writing from the imagination and observation it conveys. One may as well try to take the wetness out of rain or strip stars of their light. So once again I will trust in example to make my point.

Anna Karenina is a magnificent work of realism. Through eight hundred and fifty pages, Leo Tolstoy tells the heartbreaking tale of a brave and beautiful woman who dares all for love and loses. He sets Anna's story in the Russia (and Italy) of his own day and peoples it with an enormous cast of characters, a dozen of whom we get to know intimately. Tolstoy, and we with him, follow their criss-crossing paths through four years in gaslit Moscow ballrooms and sunlit fields on vast country estates. The illusion of realism in *Anna Karenina* is flawless, believable in every detail and every emotion. Tolstoy blends imagination and observation perfectly. He uses imagination's first *if* to create his characters and the fourth to watch them from a moveable point of view; all they do he creates from profound observation of what life is like and how humans act. Anna, Karenin, Vronsky, Kitty, Levin, and Oblonsky, imaginary though they be, live in *Anna Karenina* quite as if they were Russians real as Tolstoy himself, men and women walking with him on the soil of the motherland.

Anna Karenina is beautifully written. The beauty of the writing begins with Tolstoy's purposeful way with words: he always chooses the simplest one that will do the job:

> She went to the far end of a little drawing room and sank into an armchair.

Tolstoy loves the rhythm of long, inclusive sentences:

> Whereupon the chemist's assistant called out in German to someone, asking if he should supply the drug, and receiving an affirmative reply from behind the partition reached down a small phial and a funnel, slowly filled it from a larger bottle, stuck on a label, sealed it, in spite of all Levin's entreaties to the contrary, and was about to wrap it up too.

and he interweaves their long, legato phrases into multivoiced harmony:

> And that most difficult task for the hostess of a small dinner-party which includes such guests as the steward and the architect—people of quite a different world, struggling not to be overawed by an elegance to which they were unaccustomed,

and unable to sustain a large share of the general conversation—Anna managed with her usual tact, naturally, and even taking pleasure in it herself, as Dolly observed.

Tolstoy uses metaphor sparely but effectively, most often to point out parallels between humans and nature—here the "crystallization of society":

> As definitely and inevitably as a drop of water exposed to the frost is transformed into a snow crystal of a certain shape, so each newcomer at the springs was immediately established in his special place.

His descriptions are dynamic and exact:

> Now and then the storm would abate for an instant, and then blow with such gusts that it seemed impossible to stand up against it. Meanwhile, people ran along chatting cheerfully together, creaking the boards of the platform and constantly opening and shutting the heavy doors. The stooping shadow of a man glided past her feet and she heard the sound of a hammer upon iron.

and his dialogue unforced:

> "Well, can we start sowing?" he asked, after a pause.
> "We might, round behind Turkino, tomorrow or the day after."
> "And the clover?"
> "I've sent Vassily and Mishka: they're sowing. Only I don't know if they'll get through, it's so muddy."

Anna Karenina is a serious book—for Anna it is a tragedy—yet Tolstoy lightens his major themes with comic touches, the foibles, for instance, of easy-going Prince Oblonsky, who "was on familiar terms with everyone with whom he took a glass of champagne, and he took a glass of champagne with everyone"; and the frustrations of Levin, as he searches earnestly after enlightenment:

> To work out the whole subject theoretically and to finish his book, which, in Levin's day-dreams, would not merely revolutionize political economy but annihilate that science altogether . . . all that was left was to make a tour abroad. . . . Levin was only waiting for the wheat to be delivered and to get the money for it before taking his departure. But rain set in . . . and even prevented delivery of the wheat.

I hear Tolstoy's voice in every sentence of *Anna Karenina*. When, occasionally, he does speak directly to the reader, I find his words wise:

> Every man who is familiar down to the last detail with all the complexities of his own circumstances . . . never supposes that other people are surrounded by just as complicated an array of personal affairs as his.

Over the length of *Anna Karenina* Tolstoy builds word resonance and rhythm into the rich reverberations of a full symphony orchestra. Every character has her or his own melody, every chapter has strong contrasts in tone, tempo, and texture. Sometimes the bass viols and tympani boom fateful *fortissimi*; at others the woodwinds and strings whisper *pianissimo* laments. Tolstoy achieves this grand word music by the most economical means, writing, in sum, like the old peasant whose work style Levin admires: scythe in hand, he steadily tackles the job before him, adaptable to its changing needs and able to look about himself as he goes:

> When he came to a hillock he would change his actions and go round the hillock with short strokes first with the point and then with the heel of the scythe. . . . [S]ometimes he would pick a wild berry and eat it or offer it to Levin; sometimes he threw a twig out of the way with the point of the steel, or examined a quail's nest, from which the hen-bird flew up from right under the scythe; or got a snake that crossed his path, lifting it on the scythe as though on a fork, showed it to Levin, and flung it away.

Yet, when I am away from *Anna Karenina*, what of all this beautiful writing do I remember word for word? Only the first sentence, the keen observation that everyone remembers, here in my own translation:

> Happy families are all alike; unhappy families are unhappy each in their own way.

The million or more words that follow fade from my mind. What I do remember is the *life* of *Anna Karenina*, the imaginary yet utterly real world the words create, the people who live in that world, and all they do and feel. I remember the biting cold of Russia's winters and the fertile warmth of her summers; I remember the crowd at the racetrack, Oblonsky and his chorus girls. I remember Kitty and Levin falling so fumblingly in love and how their love grows in strength and tenderness through the death of Levin's brother and the birth of their first child. I remember Karenin, the hard-hearted husband, and Vronsky, the vain young lover. Above all I remember Anna, beautiful, courageous Anna, drifting in a fog of hurt and confusion to her lonely suicide.

This life I remember is more than the writing of *Anna Karenina*; it is the living thought Tolstoy conveys through the writing, energy that bursts from the words of the book and convinces me utterly of its truth to life. Yes, the writing is beautiful. Were it less so, perhaps the thought it conveys would be less vibrant and memorable. Yet I love the writing of *Anna Karenina* more for the life it brings me than for itself. I love the writing for all that Tolstoy gives me through it of his own knowledge and fancy, for all the colors, tastes, and smells it evokes, for the laughter and the tears that linger long after its words are gone.

The observation, imagination, and writing skill realists need to rope the stallion have matching motives that keep them at their self-appointed task. Realists enjoy observing and describing life. They get pleasure from following imagination where it leads, and, despite the difficulty, they like the trial and error process of improving writing ability. A fourth motive too, I think, spurs realists on: the hope of fame.

Readers are dear to all writers. Every writer wants to be read by as many people as possible; each knows he or she competes with scores of fellow scribblers for the eyes and mind of the general public. What do readers most want to read? What will attract their attention, interest, and favor? Realists bet that truth from life has the best chance to attract the largest audience. This is what they want from books; this, they figure, is what we all are looking for in the many signals of social intercourse. Realism connects fiction to the practical need for good information; unrealism is as useless as an instruction manual that tells us to put the cart before the horse. Readers can learn from realism. C. S. Forester's Horatio Hornblower series, for example, makes fascinating drama of English naval tactics during the Napoleonic blockade, and Raymond Chandler's counterfeit coin plot in *The High Window* entails a precise description of lost wax casting:

> A small opening is left from the wax to outside by attaching a steel pin which is withdrawn when the cement sets. Then the crystabolite casting is cooked over a flame until the wax boils out through this small opening, leaving a hollow mold of the original model. This is clamped against a crucible on a centrifuge and molten gold is shot into it by centrifugal force from the crucible.

Realism, in sum, provides a service to its readers as well as entertaining them. Realists hope that the information conveyed will add to the appeal of their work: if the fiction falls flat, it will at least have the ground of fact to land on.

Writers worth their salt hope for more than passing fame; they send their mark ahead to times and generations they will never see. What makes writing endure? Close connection to life, hopes the realist. If that is the best bet today, it will be tomorrow as well. Truths of nature and character persist in time; sticking to them is the secret of artistic self-renewal. We can see ourselves in Oedipus, Hamlet, and Willy Loman, and every year, year after year, "rough winds do shake the darling buds of May." This hope, that captive life will keep his work alive, more than any other keeps a realist steadily stalking the wild horse. For if, by hook or crook, he can get his string of words around the proud beast's neck and climb aboard its bucking back, why then the steed will carry him galloping down through the centuries on clattering hooves!

So realists try and try again. They sit at their desks and stare at the white page. What added black will paint the seedy clientele of La Tupinamba, a garish bar in Mexico City?

> It was about nine o'clock at night, and the place was pretty full with bullfight managers, agents, newspapermen, pimps, cops, and almost everybody you can think of, except somebody you would trust with your watch.
>
> James M. Cain, *Serenade*

Or a French coal-mining village seen by a young man as he walks into it hungry and alone in pitchblack night?

> And yet here on this naked plain, in this thick darkness, he had a feeling of hesitation; Le Voreux struck fear into him. Each squall seemed fiercer than the last, as though each time it blew from a more distant horizon. No sign of dawn; the sky was dead: only the furnaces and coke ovens glared and reddened the shadows, but did not penetrate their mystery. And huddled in its lair like some evil beast, Le Voreux crouched even lower and its breath came in longer and deeper gasps, as though it were struggling to digest its meal of human flesh.
>
> Émile Zola, *Germinal*

Or a mysterious detective who "was born to be a secret"?

> He was a short, dried-up, withered old man who seemed to have secreted his very blood; for nobody would have given him credit for the possession of six ounces of it in his whole body.

How he lived was a secret; where he lived was a secret; and even what he was, was a secret. In his musty old pocketbook he carried contradictory cards, in some of which he called himself a coal-merchant, in others a wine-merchant, in others a commission agent, in others a collector, in others an accountant: as if he didn't know the secret himself.

Dickens, *Martin Chuzzlewit*

Certain patterns realists make over and over again: "he said," "she said," "it was," "by then," and "the," a million times "the." The words threaten to fall apart into scrambled letters:

Van looked at his love's inclined neck as she played anagrams with Grace, who had innocently suggested "insect."

"Scient," said Ada, writing it down.

"Oh no!" objected Grace.

"Oh yes! I'm sure it exists. He is a great scient. Dr. Entsic was a scient in insects."

Grace meditated, tapping her puckered brow with the eraser end of the pencil and came up with:

"Nicest!"

"Incest," said Ada instantly.

"I give up," said Grace. "We need a dictionary to check your little inventions."

Vladimir Nabokov, *Ada*

Realists push on undaunted, cementing one word beside another and reaching for the next. Their glue? The private decision to mark just so, each writer's personal, passionate conviction that only this word and then that word will tell the story as it must be told, will make real worlds and real people leap off the page into the minds and hearts of millions of readers.

All realists know, however, that as they struggle to get life on the page, scratching their heads and scratching out their mistakes, life goes on inside and outside their windows in an unending welter whose stupendous sum no realist will ever reckon. At the end of *The Anatomy Lesson* Philip Roth shows his writer Zuckerman, older if not wiser than he was in *The Ghost Writer*, running away from his desk plagued by inexplicable paralyzing pain. His search for a cure takes him to a huge Chicago hospital where he plunges his arms and face deep into the hampers of blood-stained laundry, desperately trying to confront life in the raw. At night he follows interns on their rounds down dimly lit corridors. "In every bed the fear was different," Zuckerman finds, "and always the enemy was wicked and real." At one bed a woman asks, "in a small compliant voice," about her surgery.

"Was it very deep, Doctor?" "We got it all," the intern told her, showing Zuckerman the long stitched up wound under the oily dressing just behind her ear. "Nothing there to worry you anymore." "Yes? Well, that's good then." "Absolutely." "And— am I going to see you again?" "You sure are," he said, squeezing her hand, and then he left her at peace on her pillow, with Zuckerman, the intern's intern in tow. What a job! The paternal bond to those in duress, the urgent immediate human exchange! All this indispensable work to be done, all this digging away at disease—and he'd given his fanatical devotion to sitting with a typewriter alone in a room!

BIBLIOGRAPHY

Writing and Life springs from years of following my nose to books I love. I hope you find your way to them too, and I guarantee that they will bring you pleasures beyond price—stories and characters you will never forget, and abiding insights into the art of writing. The books I chose to illustrate my points make, of course, an arbitrary list. Another writer or I myself in a different mood could have chosen dozens of other and equally valuable works.

With the exception of Foerster and Steadman's *Writing and Thinking*, a college text from the 1930s that I found in a used bookshop in Berkeley, California, all these books should be easy to find. Most of the editions listed below are widely available paperbacks, but do not labor long and hard to locate the exact one I cite. Grab the one you find first and enjoy it. The book's the thing, not where one editor puts the commas or whether one translator decided on "too" for "*aussi*" and another chose "also."

Jane Austen. *Pride and Prejudice*. New York: Washington Square Press, 1960.

———.*Emma*. New York: New American Library, 1964.

Honore Balzac. *Pére Goriot*, trans. Burton Raffel. New York: W. W. Norton & Company, 1994.

Ray Bradbury. *The Martian Chronicles*. New York: Bantam Books, 1974.

Charlotte Brontë. *Jane Eyre*. New York: Random House, 1943.

John Bunyan. *The Pilgrim's Progress*. New York: New American Library, 1964.

James M. Cain. *Serenade*. New York: Vintage Books, 1978; originally published by Alfred A. Knopf, Inc., 1937.

Thomas Carlyle. *Sartor Resartus and On Heroes, Hero Worship and the Heroic*, Lecture III, "The Hero as Poet." New York: Everyman's Library, 1973.

Lewis Carroll. *Alice's Adventures in Wonderland & Through the Looking Glass*. New York: New American Library, 1960.

Miguel Cervantes. *Don Quixote*, trans. Walter Starkie. New York: New American Library, 1979.

Raymond Chandler. *The Big Sleep*. New York: Ballantine Books, 1971; originally published by Alfred A. Knopf, Inc., 1939.

———. *The High Window*. New York: Pocket Books, 1945; originally published by Alfred A. Knopf, Inc., 1942.

Daniel Defoe. *Robinson Crusoe*. New York: Bantam Books, 1991.

Charles Dickens. *Martin Chuzzlewit*. Baltimore: Penguin Books, 1968.

———. *Bleak House*. Boston: Houghton Mifflin, 1956.

———. *A Tale of Two Cities*. New York: Modern Library, 1950.

Isak Dinesen. *Out of Africa*. New York: Vintage Books, 1985; originally published by Random House, 1937.

Fyodor Dostoyevsky. *Crime and Punishment*, trans. Constance Garnett. New York: Modern Library, 1950.

———. *The Idiot*, trans. David Magarshack. Penguin Books, 1955.

A. Conan Doyle. *Sherlock Holmes: The Complete Novels and Stories*, vols. 1 and 2. New York: Bantam Books, 1986.

Theodore Dreiser. *Trilogy of Desire (The Financier, The Titan, The Stoic)*. New York: Apollo Editions, 1974.

George Elliot. *The Mill on the Floss*. New York: New American Library, 1965.

Ralph Waldo Emerson. "Spiritual Laws," from *Essays, First Series*. Boston and New York: Houghton Mifflin, 1903.

———. "Shakespeare, or The Poet," from *Representative Men*. Boston and New York: Houghton Mifflin, 1903.

Henry Fielding. *Tom Jones*. Baltimore: Penguin Books, 1966.

Norman Foerster and J. M. Steadman, Jr. *Writing and Thinking*. Boston: Houghton Mifflin, 1931.

Dashiell Hammett. *The Glass Key*. New York: Vintage Books, 1972; originally published by Alfred A. Knopf, Inc., 1931.

Thomas Hardy. *The Return of the Native*. New York: Doubleday & Co., Inc., undated.

Holy Bible. *Psalms, Gospel of St. Matthew, Gospel of St. Mark, Gospel of St. Luke, Gospel of St. John*. Authorized (King James) Version. Nashville: The Gideons International, 1964.

Homer. *The Odyssey*, trans. E. V. Rieu. Baltimore: Penguin Books, 1946.

Victor Hugo. *The Hunchback of Notre Dame* (no trans. named). New York: Dodd Mead & Company, 1947.

Michael Innes. *From London Far*. London: Penguin Books, 1946.

Thomas Jefferson et al. *Declaration of Independence*.

Samuel Johnson. "Preface to the Edition of Shakespeare's Plays," from *Samuel Johnson on Shakespeare*. London: Penguin Books, 1989.

James Jones. *Go to the Widowmaker*. New York: Dell Books, 1968; originally published by Delacorte Press, 1967.

Franz Kafka. "Metamorphosis," from *The Penal Colony, Stories and Short Pieces*. New York. Schocken Books, 1948.

Stephen King. *The Shining*. New York: New American Library-Dutton, 1970.

Herman Melville. *Moby Dick*. New York: Signet Classics, 1961.

John Milton. *Paradise Lost*, from *The Complete Poetry and Selected Prose of John Milton*. New York: Modern Library, 1950.

Vladimir Nabokov. *Lolita*. New York: Berkeley Medallion, 1966; originally published by Olympia Press, 1955, and G. P. Putnam's Sons, 1958.

———. *Ada or Ardor: A Family Chronicle*. New York: McGraw-Hill Book Company, 1969.

Ogden Nash. *You Can't Get There from Here*. Boston: Little, Brown and Company, 1957.

George Orwell. *Burmese Days*. New York: Harcourt Brace, 1950.

Thomas Paine. *Common Sense and The Rights of Man*. New York: New American Library, 1984.

Walter Piston. *Counterpoint*. New York: W. W. Norton & Co., Inc., 1947.

Willard Van Orman Quine. *Methods of Logic*. New York: Holt, Rinehart and Winston, 1959.

Philip Roth. *The Ghost Writer*. New York: Farrar, Straus and Giroux, 1979.

———. *The Anatomy Lesson*. New York: Farrar, Straus and Giroux, 1983.

Roger Sessions. *The Musical Experience of Composer, Performer, and Listener*. Princeton: Princeton University Press, 1950.

William Shakespeare. *Sonnets, Romeo and Juliet, Macbeth, Hamlet,*

King Lear, Henry V, Julius Caesar, from *William Shakespeare: The Complete Works.* Baltimore: Penguin Books, 1969.

Alexander Solzhenitsyn. *One Day in the Life of Ivan Denisovich,* trans. Max Hayward and Ronald Hingley. New York: Bantam Books; originally published by Frederick A. Praeger, Inc., 1963.

Lawrence Sterne. *Tristram Shandy.* New York: Modern Library, undated.

Jonathan Swift. *Gulliver's Travels.* Boston: Houghton Mifflin, 1960.

Leo Tolstoy. *Anna Karenina,* trans. Rosemary Edmonds. London: Penguin Books, 1954.

Anthony Trollope. *The Last Chronicle of Barset.* New York: Viking Penguin, 1981.

———. *Can You Forgive Her?* Oxford: Oxford University Press, 1973.

Mark Twain. *The Adventures of Huckleberry Finn.* New York: Bantam Books, 1981.

E. B. White. *Charlotte's Web.* New York: Harper Collins, 1952.

Walt Whitman. "Crossing Brooklyn Ferry," from *Leaves of Grass,* in *The Portable Walt Whitman.* New York: The Viking Press, 1945.

Ludwig Wittgenstein. *Philosophical Investigations.* New York: The Macmillan Company, 1958.

Emile Zola. *Germinal,* trans. L. W. Tancock. Baltimore: Penguin Books, 1954.

UNIVERSITY PRESS OF NEW ENGLAND publishes books under its own imprint and is the publisher for Brandeis University Press, Dartmouth College, Middlebury College Press, University of New Hampshire, University of Rhode Island, Tufts University, University of Vermont, Wesleyan University Press, and Salzburg Seminar.

ABOUT THE AUTHOR

Michael Lydon is a writer and musician who lives in New York City. Author of three books, *Rock Folk*, *Boogie Lightning*, and *How to Succeed in Show Business by Really Trying*, Lydon has written for many periodicals as well, *The Atlantic Monthly*, *The New York Times Magazine* and *Book Review*, *Rolling Stone*, and *The Village Voice* among them. He is also a songwriter and, with Ellen Mandel, has composed an opera, *Passion in Pigskin*. A graduate of Yale University, Lydon is a member of ASCAP.

LIBRARY OF CONGRESS CATALOGING-IN-PUBLICATION DATA

Lydon, Michael.
    Writing and life / by Michael Lydon.
       p.   cm.
    Includes bibliographical references.
    ISBN 0–87451–730–3 (alk. paper)
    1. Authorship.   I. Title.
PN151.L94   1995
808′.02 — dc20   95–13843